GILA MONSTER

Woman displaying two Gila monsters about 1900. Photo courtesy
Central Arizona Historical Society, Phoenix.

GILA MONSTER

Facts and Folklore of America's Aztec Lizard

~ ~ ~ ~ ~ ~ ~ ~

by

David E. Brown and Neil B. Carmony

~ ~ ~ ~ ~ ~ ~ ~

~ ~ ~ ~ ~ ~ ~ ~

Cover photos, drawings, and maps by Randy Babb

~ ~ ~ ~ ~ ~ ~ ~

~ ~ ~ ~ ~ ~ ~ ~

High-Lonesome Books
Silver City, New Mexico
88062

~ ~ ~ ~ ~ ~ ~ ~

ISBN # 0-944383-18-1

Library of Congress Catalog Card # 91-075930

~ ~ ~ ~ ~ ~ ~ ~

Second Edition

~ ~ ~ ~ ~ ~ ~ ~

DEDICATION

To Louella, who made it happen

FOREWORD

Few animals have had a greater fascination for man than the Gila monster *(Heloderma suspectum)* and the Mexican beaded lizard *(Heloderma horridum)*. The classic works of Bogert and Del Campo (1956) and Loeb (1913) and some 400 additional pieces of literature have been examined and put in a very readable form herein by the authors. *Gila Monster* considers the lizard's natural history, including descriptions, fossil records, distribution, temperature and moisture regulation, reproduction, longevity, enemies, and population status; its relationship to humans and folklore; its venom; bites on humans and other animals, bite treatment, and a section on references, among other related topics. After studying this animal for almost 50 years, I found the text crammed with interesting and important data, and it reads as smooth as a Klauber.

Findlay E. Russell, M.D., Ph.D.
Professor of Health Sciences
University of Arizona

TABLE OF CONTENTS

LIST OF ILLUSTRATIONS

i

Maps

PREFACE

J. B. Lemmon, the botanist, has been in Arizona, and brought with him on his return to Oakland, a curious reptile. It was captured near Phoenix by a chief of the Maricopa Indians, by the aid of a small lasso made from a pocket rope. It is called the "Aztec Lizard" or Heloderma Suspectum, is 19 inches long, six inches around the body, has a thick tail like a kangaroo and weighs two pounds. Its color is yellow, with clearly defined black scales one-eighth of an inch in diameter, resembling the markings on the wing of a butterfly... It is slow-motioned, cannot overtake its prey, and is consequently easily devoured by its enemies; hence its liability to become extinct, which enhances the value of the few specimens in existence...

Phoenix Herald, June 18, 1880

There is something about seeing your first wild Gila monster that makes for a lasting impression. At least it was so with me. It was a bright spring morning in 1962 while I was visiting a mesquite forest along the Gila River now drowned by the filling of Painted Rock Reservoir. I had only recently been hired by the Arizona Game and Fish Department as the wildlife manager for Gila Bend -- a small town jokingly referred to as the fan-belt capital of the world because of its 120 degree summers and desert location on the highway between Yuma and Phoenix. Then as now not much was going on in Gila Bend and three of us had decided to spend the day looking for the old Butterfield Stage route and poking around Indian ruins.

While puzzling over the meaning of a series of pictographs on an outcrop of rock near the river, we were greeted by a Halloween-colored creature lumbering toward us. Although I had never seen a Gila monster before, I had no doubt what the creature was. Its colors and markings were similar to those of a monarch butterfly, and the animal's pebbly texture and oddly purposeful gait were exactly what I had been told to expect.

Now, a meeting with a Gila monster commands more than just attention. The urge to pick up one of these slow-moving oddities exerts about the same power as the fear of doing so. Knowing of the animal's venomous character, but beset by an irresistable temptation to handle such a bizarre and easily captured creature, I stood there, debating what to do. My comrades, however, had other intentions. It took me but a moment to realize that they were busily engaged in searching for

1

appropriate missiles to stone the monster into oblivion lest at some future date, "it might bite some innocent child!"

Wanting neither any injury to come to such an inoffensive beast, nor to have to give my companions a citation for harming one of the state's only two protected reptiles, I could resist no longer. Grasping the lizard firmly behind the head, I retrieved Mr. Gila monster from further debate and vowed to release the dangerous brute in a more remote corner of the globe. My real intent, however, was to take it home for further examination. The creature had only three legs and was without even the vestige of a stub where its left front appendage should have been. My curiosity was piqued.

I was surprised at its quickness once the animal got over its initial hissing and fright. The handicap of a missing leg had little effect on its agility. Had I known this, I might not have been so rash as to pick the animal up in the first place. Carefully wrapping my charge in a burlap sack, I took the Gila monster home while my accomplices continued their search for mislaid arrowheads and vanished stagecoach stations.

That night I broke a hen's egg in an ash tray and placed it and the Gila monster in a cardboard carton. I had neither the heart to turn such a fascinating creature into a pickled specimen for science nor a desire to be burdened with the care of a reluctant captive. Tomorrow I would return the lizard to his home in the mesquite *bosque* with a full stomach to compensate for interrupting whatever business it was so intent on pursuing.

When I awoke the sun was already illuminating the walls of my small bachelor apartment. Leaning over on my floor-bound mattress, I peered over into the box to check on my charge. Only an empty ashtray was there. The apartment had just one room and both doors were closed. I dared not move. The night had been cool and I *knew* the Gila monster was warming his body somewhere in the bedding. I could feel the flicking black tongue in a dozen different places and imagined those needle-like teeth would soon be imbedded somewhere in my anatomy. Once the jaws of a Gila monster clamp down, I had been warned, you have the devil to pay to break his hold.

I lay still for the longest time...waiting for the slightest movement, the faintest touch, anything to inform me of the animal's whereabouts. Sweat was exuding from every pore. What would be the Gila monster's response to moisture?

It was then that I heard the scratching. I wished that I had moveable ears like a deer so that I could pinpoint the source of the sound. Gradually it came to me that the noise was the pawing of claws on metal. My awakening nightmare was in the shower stall. I was saved.

Two hours later a three-legged Gila monster was burrowing its way into a packrat nest under a mesquite tree below Indian pictographs. We would never meet again.

In the ensuing years I have come upon no more than two dozen Gila monsters -- few enough to always be a surprise, but more than most Arizonans. For five years running I never saw one; in 1990 I happened on to four. With two exceptions -- one basking in February sunshine, and an August visitor to a camp in the grasslands of the Altar Valley on the Arizona-Sonora border -- these sightings have all been in the spring or early summer. Most of them occurred in the paloverde and saguaro-studded hillsides of the Sonoran Desert, three were in mesquite thickets, and one in the Chihuahuan Desert near where the Gila River enters Arizona from New Mexico.

My co-author has only seen five Gila monsters in a lifetime of living in the Southwest. Four of his were along river bottoms and another was a youngster trapped in a friend's patio east of Tucson near Saguaro National Monument. Most of his encounters were in September. All of which goes to show how few of these reptiles are seen and how limited the information gleaned from any one person's observations must be.

No wonder then, that every Gila monster meeting is regarded as a serendipitous occasion, one guaranteed to make any day afield more memorable. And, while I may attempt a photograph, I no longer feel the need to pick one up. Nor do my friends want to throw stones at them. We all agree that these desert dwellers are best left alone to go about their business. That, I think, is very tangible progress indeed.

David E. Brown

INTRODUCTION

I've seed a lizzard what could out-pizen any frog or toad in
the world...went after it with a stick, but the thunderin' thing,
instead of runnin' away like any nateral lizzard, squatted on
its tail and spit at me. It were about three feet long, and it
had yaller scales all over it, like an alligator's hide, and it were
the the hardest critter to kill I ever heard tell on. I knocked it
over and beat it with a club until my arm ached, but I might as
well have tried to cut down a mesquit tree with a blade of
grass...the blasted lizzard never stopped spittin.' I jerked out
my revolver and fired four shots at it, but the balls all skipped
off its tarnal hide back into the river, and at last I got it so
mad I shook the pistol in the critter's face, and I'm a liar if it
didn't jump at it and ketch the muzzle in its mouth, and
what's more I couldn't git it away again. I pulled, and jerked,
and sweat and swore, but no use; and I believe Mister Lizzard
would hev pulled me plum into the river if I hadn't thought to
cock the revolver and shoot it down his throat. The shot blew
the body clean in two, and then I hope to die if the head and
fore legs didn't get the pistol away from me, into the river
and swim away with it.

"The Gila Monster," *The World* (San Diego), Feb. 20,
1873

With the possible exception of the vampire bat, no North American
animal has been the source of more superstitions, the subject of as many
legends, or the object of more exaggerated claims than the Gila
monster. That the lizard's poisonous properties were debated by
scientists for years is only one aspect of a bizarre legacy that continues
to this day. The purpose of the Gila monster's venom is still hotly
argued by biologists and laymen alike, as is the reason for the reptile's
jaguar-like coloration. Not only is the Gila monster America's largest
and only poisonous lizard, it is our slowest moving saurian, the only
reptile having an armored hide, and the only lizard with a forked tongue
like a snake's. No biologist has yet discovered a Gila monster nest or
observed a Gila monster hatching in the wild. Add to these phenomena
the fact that more than 99% of the Gila monster's life is spent out of
sight below the surface of the ground and you have the makings for a
very mysterious creature indeed. But then, the reptile's secretive ways
have always been an important facet of the animal's appeal to
storytellers and biologists alike.

5

Although people almost everywhere have heard of Gila monsters, few have had the opportunity to see one in its natural habitat. The creature is rare in California and Nevada, and highly localized in Utah and New Mexico. Even within its stronghold in the Sonoran Desert of Arizona and Sonora, Mexico, where the animal is as characteristic a species as the saguaro cactus, the Gila monster is seldom seen by those who do not make it their business to seek him out.

Perhaps the most unusual aspect of the Gila monster story, however, is our progressive change in attitude toward this unusual desert denizen. Feared by Indians and Hispanics, villified by early American settlers, the Gila monster has in turn been regarded as a creature of dread and loathing, a pest to be killed at every opportunity, and a marketable curio for commercial exploitation. Happily, it is now valued as an object of scientific study and increasingly appreciated as an interesting inhabitant of our rapidly-changing Southwest that should be preserved for posterity.

All of which we think makes for a story worth telling. We hope you agree.

PART I NATURAL HISTORY OF GILA MONSTERS

The Gila monster stalked his prey with infinite patience. His beaded body literally hugging the desert sand, he crept within striking distance. With a sudden lunge and click of powerful jaws he snapped at a packrat -- too late. The rat scurried away. The Gila monster hissed in frustrated rage and one drop of saliva fell from its mouth to the ground.

The spot where the Gila monster left that one drop of saliva can still be seen in the desert today, 10 years later. All vegetation for a radius of 10 yards withered and died immediately and none new has ever grown here. For months afterwards any animal who ventured within this circle died on the spot, and the area is littered with skeletons of unfortunate rats, lizards, birds and snakes.

> H. R. Moore, "Gila Monster -- Boris Karloff of the Desert," 1959.

DISCOVERY BY SCIENCE

Indian and Mexican residents of Sonora and early Arizona had long been acquainted with the Gila monster, but it was not until an 1869 meeting of the Academy of Natural Sciences of Philadelphia that Professor Edward Drinker Cope first formally described the reptile as a "new" species. Cope had noticed that a large lizard collected by Arthur Schott in 1855 during a survey of the U. S.- Mexico boundary had been misidentified despite a rather good likeness of the animal accompanying the report on his specimen (Fig. 1). Erroneously labeled by the Smithsonian Institution as *Heloderma horridum*, Schott's animal had a greater number of scales on the head and body, a shorter tail, and a markedly different color pattern than the Mexican reptile which had been known since the 17th Century as the *Acaltetepon* or Aztec lizard.

Cope gave his new species the Latin name of *Heloderma suspectum*. The animal was obviously a close relative of the Aztec lizard, which a German herpetologist had described in 1829 as *Heloderma horridum* and which is now popularly called the Mexican beaded lizard. The generic word *Heloderma* is from the Greek words *helos* for the head of a nail or stud and *derma* for skin; thus *Heloderma* appropriately means studded skin. The last or species name, *suspectum*, was applied to the new species because Cope suspected, on the basis of its grooved teeth and reputation, that the lizard *might* be poisonous.

Figure 1. First scientific drawing of a Gila monster. Copied from Baird, 1859, courtesy Arizona Historical Society, Tucson.

COMMON NAMES

The origin of the name "Gila monster" is uncertain, but the term comes into general usage shortly after the Civil War when large numbers of Americans began arriving in the Southwest. The earliest use of the name in print that we have found is in 1873, and articles in the 1870's apply the term as if it had been in use for some time. The "Gila" appellation is almost certainly due to the lizard originally being most often encountered along the Gila River, but there is a remote possibility that the designation was derived from the phonetically similar scientific term of "Heloderma" or "Heloderm." The colorful term of "monster" is presumably due to the lizard's ferocious appearance and large size as lizards go. Certainly "monster" is not an inappropriate image, if one imagines viewing the reptile's gaping mouth head-on from the perspective of a helpless baby rabbit, bird or other intended victim!

Both the Mexican beaded lizard and Gila monster are called *escorpión* in Mexico and by Mexican-Americans. This designation is thought by some to have originated from a corruption of the Spanish word *escupir*, to spit, because of the erroneous belief in Mexico that the lizard spits its venom. The word *escorpión* is also used to describe any of several venomous animals, including the scorpion, which in Mexico is more commonly called *alacrán*. Should a need to differentiate between the two species of *Heloderma* arise, Mexicans will also sometimes use the contrived name of *Gila monstruo* to indicate the *escorpión*'s northern cousin.

DESCRIPTION

Antonio Romero, Jr., caught a magnificent specimen of the Gila monster on his father's ranch in west Yuma yesterday morning. The beauty is 14 inches in length and when it puts on its "swells" it is about as large around as a woman's wrist. Its head resembles that of the large grey rattlesnake, but it is very black. Its eyes sparkle like diamonds, especially when it is mad. Its body is pale rose or flesh color, dotted, spotted, striped and embellished with jet black, and resembling the painting on an Indian basket or on an olla. It opens its mouth, which inside is a bluish pink, like an alligator. It drinks water like an old toper, is very lively and ready to fight when once molested or stirred up. It has long, crooked, sharp claws on its feet which it extends at will like a cat. Its hind legs are put on hind-side before, and wrong side up, but for all this it can use them with great skill. Taken all and all it is one of the finest specimens of the animal that we have ever seen...

Arizona Sentinel (Yuma), June, 18, 1892

General Appearance: The Gila monster has been variously described as "hideous," "beautiful," "loathsome," "artistic," "uncommonly ugly," "pleasant appearing," "disgusting," "most attractive," "unattractive," "repulsive," and "colorful." Truly, beauty is in the eye of the beholder.

Most people recognize a Gila monster on first sight, or think they do, whether they are familiar with the animal or not. Surely no other lizard lumbers along in Halloween-hued skin the texture of Indian corn. Also making for ready identification are the lizard's elongated body, robust tail, large flattened head protuding from a short neck, short spindly legs, and feet with five toes of nearly equal length that look remarkably like little human hands.

9

Closer examination reveals that the animal's snout is black as are much of the feet and the forked tongue that periodically flicks in and out. On most specimens, a pattern of black or dark brown blotches overlays a lighter "background" that is most often a shade of orange, but may be yellow, flesh-colored, cream, or salmon. The tail, which comprises from 40 to just over 50 percent of the length of the body, is alternately marked with four or five black bands. The markings are never the same on any two individuals -- each Gila monster is unique.

The "beadwork" effect is produced by special rounded scales, each covering a particle of bone, or osteoderm (bony skin). These osteoderms are so closely embedded in the skin covering the head, back, sides, legs, and tail, that the reptile's hide is almost impervious to being cut or punctured. Although such protective bony structures were common in the skins of dinosaurs, the Gila monster and Mexican beaded lizard are the only living reptiles making extensive use of this type of armor. More conventional scales cover the animal's light-colored underside. Unlike snakes and a few other lizards, the skin is not shed whole but in small patches. The relatively small eyes are dark brown, almost black, and the pupils are round and bird-like rather than eliptical as in some reptiles. The cloaca or anal opening is normally concealed by scales and not always apparent, a feature that no doubt explains the popular misconception that the Gila monster has no anus (Fig. 2). The claws are sharply curved and straw-colored.

When the inside of the generous, mostly purplish-black mouth is displayed, a not infrequent defensive posture, the Gila monster's massive light-colored jaw muscles become visible. Should one risk pulling down on one of the animal's bulging lower lips, exposing the fleshy gums, some of the monster's up to one-fourth-inch teeth will "erupt" like shards of glass (Fig. 3). Both the upper and lower jaws are so armed; each side of the lower jaw has a full complement of nine or ten teeth, and each side of the upper jaw contains eight or nine main teeth plus four small pre-maxillary or front teeth (Fig. 4). The leading edges of the large curved teeth in the middle of the lower jaw have distinct grooves (Fig. 5); all of the teeth are poorly anchored and are alternately replaced by the eruption of new teeth throughout the animal's life.

No difference exists in either the color or the markings of males and females, and the sex of a Gila monster cannot always be determined with certainty by external features. Mature males, however, tend to be larger and have a wider head and a squarer build than adult females, which tend to have a more oval body shape than most males. Some biologists have also reported that the tails of males are proportionally a trifle longer than those of similarly-aged females.

Figure 2. Underside of a Gila monster with the nearly-invisible vent closed (top), and open (bottom).

Figure 3. Exposed teeth of a Gila monster.

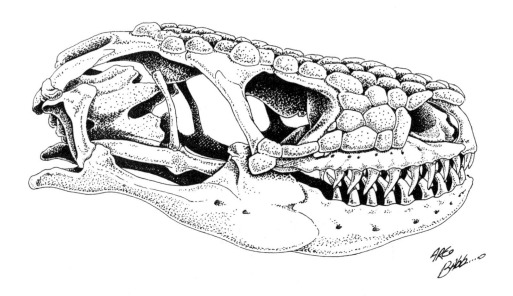

Figure 4. Skull of a Gila monster.

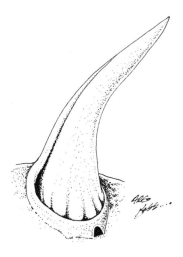

Figure 5. Enlarged view of a Gila monster tooth showing anterior groove.

13

Hatchlings are lighter in color than the adults, the yellow-orange markings are more cream-colored, and the dark markings give them a distinctly banded appearance (Fig. 6). The sizes, colors, and patterns of juvenile Gila monsters range between those of the hatchlings and the adults. No color or pattern changes occur after the lizard reaches maturity. Nor do Gila monsters change color under emotional stress or when placed on different backgrounds, as do chameleons, horned lizards, and some other reptiles.

The purpose of the Gila monster's striking color pattern is a puzzle and a source of controversy. Some believe that the black and orange coloration serves to identify the animal to potential predators and warm them that it is dangerous. But if so, how do predators "know" that the Gila monster is poisonous? To an uneducated predator, such colors could also be an attraction. Certainly the far greater number of coyotes, bobcats, hawks, and other predators cannot be taught that an encounter with a Gila monster is unhealthy without being bitten at least once. A defensive strategy theory is also confounded by the Gila monster's vice-like bite, which requires considerable effort to dislodge, and may come at considerable cost to the Gila monster. There are far too many predators for Gila monsters to sacrifice themselves in order to teach each predator that black-and-orange means danger.

Other people have gone to great lengths to show that the jet black muzzle and broken orange and black color pattern are excellent camouflage for an animal who spends much of its time peering out of a burrow and whose infrequent forays overland may be across pebbly, rose-colored surfaces dappled by the shadows of desert vegetation. But would not such a purpose be even better served if the animal were more cryptically colored like other lizards? It has been determined that raptors, and possibly the coyote, *can* distinguish colors, and the camouflage argument is negated whenever this lizard is seen out in the open -- the Gila monster's colors are striking. Are the colors meant to serve both functions as still others claim? The Gila monster isn't saying.

Lengths and Weights: The Gila monster is the largest lizard or "saurian" native to the United States (alligators are not considered lizards but crocodilians). Most Gila monsters take from four to five years to reach sexual maturity, at which time they are between 14 and 16 inches in length and weigh from about a pound to a pound and a half, depending upon the monster's condition, and the time of its last meal. An exceptionally large specimen will approach 20 inches and may weigh up to two pounds or more. Hatchlings are about six to six and one-half inches long and weigh just over an ounce.

Overfed captives and a few wild Gila monsters may be larger than the above figures. A specimen turned in to the Arizona Game and Fish Department's Adobe Mountain Wildlife Rehabilitation Center in 1990 was 22 1/2 inches long, thus beating the former "verified record" of 21 3/4 inches. Two-foot animals are nonetheless commonly reported in popular articles. Arizona pioneer John Spring wrote in 1889 that he had one measuring 28 inches. Even larger specimens, some up to three and one-half feet, are mentioned in old newspaper and magazine accounts, but none can compete with the fabled Castle Dome Gila monster:

> ...A few years ago...we will not attempt to say how many -- Mr. Dan Conner and a man named Pilgrim were prospecting in the Castle Dome mountains, and captured a Gila monster of prodigious size. Securing it with small cords they returned to camp for larger ropes with which to safely bind and transport their catch. When they got back to where they had left the monster they could find no trace of him. According to their story it weighed three hundred pounds. Mr. Pilgrim has long since passed to that land from which no affidavits return, but Mr. Conner still ornaments the foot-stool in the capacity of engineer for the C.S.N. Co., and he stands pledged to knock any man down on sight who mentions the subject to him...

> *Arizona Sentinel* (Yuma), September 15, 1883

Upon being questioned on the authenticity of its account by the rival *Arizona Citizen* in Tucson, the *Sentinel* responded in a follow-up column:

> The *Citizen* is not satisfied with the *Sentinel*'s Gila monster story. The editor of that paper wants us to give him something authentic, in fact, he asks how large a Gila monster we have seen. Well, if a three hundred pound Gila monster is not a sufficiently authentic reptile we will endeavor to find a heavier subject for our Tucson contemporary. We have never seen as big a one as Dan Conner, but then -- we have seen Dan Conner, and on his return will secure a sketch made on the spot of the beautiful Gila monster mentioned, and have him make affidavit before a notary as to the reptile's complexion,

weight, color of eyes, and enter into all the minute detail of this most wonderful bird, vulgarly termed a Gila monster. The sketch will be attached to the affidavit and forwarded to Tucson for examination.

Arizona Sentinel, September, 29, 1883

In view of the fact that no affidavit was forthcoming, the record weight of a Gila monster must stand as an obese four and three-fourths pound captive owned by a man named Hewitt and reported by Max Hensley in the Transactions of the Kansas Academy of Science in 1950.

Locomotion: Gila monsters are the slowest of lizards and their pace can be described as only a purposeful waddle under normal conditions, and a hurried amble when pressed. The alternate movement of the feet give the animal a peculiar rolling gait, each foreleg moving in synchrony with the opposite rear leg. Like crocodiles, the Gila monster holds its belly above the ground when traveling, as well as the heavy tail. If surprised or confronted, the Gila monster's usual response, when not totally ignoring the intrusion, is to retreat backwards, using the same alternate pattern of steps. Should escape appear unlikely, the Gila monster backs into a rock or other hard surface and curls into a semicircle where it holds its ground huffing and hissing with mouth agape. The Gila monster may lunge at an adversary who gets too close, but it does not "jump up or spring" as some writers would have you believe.

Spoor: The sharp curved claws, nearly uniformly-sized toes, and its peculiar lumbering gait make the Gila monster's tracks recognizable in sand or mud (Fig. 7). These characteristic footprints, along with the animal's scats, have enabled reptile hunters and researchers to locate Gila monsters for capture and study. The droppings are produced irregularly, ranging in captive animals fed hen eggs from once a day to once a week; presumably the interval in wild animals is even greater. Fresh droppings of egg-feeding monsters are cylindrical or conical doughy masses, whitish, tinged with yellow-green, and segmented like the rattles of a rattlesnake. If the segments have not dried and separated into individual discs, the scats are from three-fourths to one inch long and about one-half inch in diameter.

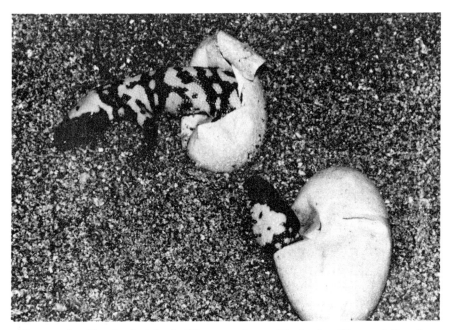

Figure 6. Newly hatched Gila monster. Photo by Howard Lawler, Arizona-Sonora Desert Museum.

Figure 7. Gila monster tracks in sand. Photo by Randy Babb.

Similar Species: Gila monsters can be readily distinguished from their close relative, the Mexican beaded lizard of western Mexico and Guatemala, by the beaded lizard's slimmer appearance and often greater size (up to three feet). Other distinguishing characteristics include the beaded lizard's darker overall coloration with a completely or nearly completely black head, its scattered yellow rather than orange or pink markings, and a longer, thinner tail that easily exceeds the length of the head and body (Fig. 8). The tail of the Mexican beaded lizard also has six or seven bands in contrast to the Gila monster's four or five. Should one care to investigate further, it will also be noted that the beaded lizard has a pink tongue, unlike the Gila monster's blackish one, as well as different numbers of certain scales and a more generous number of tail vertebrae.

Occasionally the brick-red and black male chuckwalla is misidentified as a Gila monster, and people commonly mistake a banded gecko for a baby Gila monster. The longer-tailed and also large chuckwalla (adults may attain a total length of 15 inches) is exclusively a rock-dwelling vegetarian and has a skin covered by small scales rather than colorful beads (Fig. 9). The much smaller (three to five inch) western banded gecko has a velvety smooth skin and the pupils of its eyes are usually vertical slits (Fig. 10).

FOSSIL HISTORY

> Somehow as yet the reptile known as the Gila Monster, has not been classified by naturalists, and they have gone as far only as to give it a name. It is called the "Halioderma" meaning the sunskinned reptile...a local naturalist...calls the Gila monster a hybrid, a production between a saurian and a snake... Its body resembles that of a lizard, while its head is that of a snake. It has a habit too, of throwing its tongue out like a snake and its bite is very poisonous and always fatal...

> *Arizona Daily Star* (Tucson), Oct. 2, 1890

The Gila monster and Mexican beaded lizard are the only living members of the Family Helodermatidae, more commonly called the Heloderms. Besides having a protective coat of armored hide, heavy skulls, and other similarities of bone structure, the Heloderms are unique in being the only lizards, living or extinct, to possess grooved teeth and venom glands.

Figure 8. Gila monster (A) compared to a Mexican beaded lizard (B).

Figure 9. Portrait of a chuckwalla showing identifying characteristics. Photo by Howard Lawler, Arizona-Sonora Desert Museum.

Figure 10. Portrait of a banded gecko showing identifying characteristics. Photo by Randy Babb.

Fossil remains of a primitive Heloderm, *Paraderma bogerti*, in the Bighorn Basin of Wyoming, indicate that Heloderms separated from their nearest relatives, the large monitor lizards of Asia, Africa, and Australia, toward the end of the Age of Dinosaurs about 70 million years ago (Fig. 11). Three more recently extinct forms -- *Lowesaurus matthewi* (the genus was named for Dr. Charles H. Lowe, Jr., a noted Gila monster authority at the University of Arizona), *Eurheloderma gallicum*, and *Heloderma texanum* -- have been discovered in North American and European fossil deposits dating back to the Age of Mammals between 20 and 35 million years ago. That fossil Heloderms have only been found in what is now temperate North America and Europe would indicate a northern origin for the Family. The present restriction of these saurians to the American Southwest and western Central America is thought to be due to past and present climatic problems brought on by decreasing temperatures during the ice ages. Despite the opinion of many biologists that Heloderms evolved in a wetter climate than is found at present, no fossil or archaeological evidence shows a shrinking range for Heloderms during the droughts and increased aridity that occurred with the retreat of the last Ice Age 10,000 years ago.

The arrival of weakly-grooved teeth with *Paraderma* and the increasing development of this feature in the later species indicate that the venomous character of Heloderms was acquired independently and not inherited from their reptilian ancestors. Why a venom delivery system should have developed in only these lizards during the Age of Mammals is intriguing. Given the tendency for many past forms to be larger than living representatives, it is also a little surprising that none of the extinct Heloderms was larger than the two living species.

RANGE AND DISTRIBUTION

The Gila monster is primarily an animal of the Sonoran Desert of Arizona and northwest Mexico and shares a range roughly coinciding with the distribution of the desert tortoise and Gambel's quail. Outlying populations extend into the Chihuahuan Desert of extreme southwest New Mexico and northward into Mohave Desert locales in southwest Utah, southern Nevada and southeast California (Map 1). Elevations from which the animal has been collected range from as low as sea-level in Sonora to elevations approximating 5,000 feet in semidesert grassland and the lower reaches of chaparral and oak woodland. Gila monsters picked up in Texas and other "out of range" localities are escaped or released captives.

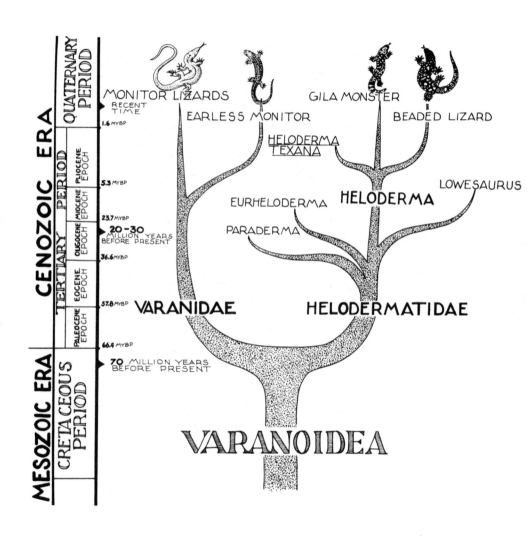

Figure 11. Evolutionary history of the Helodermatids.

Map 1. Distributions of the Gila monster and Mexican beaded lizard.

Arizona: The great majority of Gila monster sightings in Arizona are in the zone of paloverde trees and saguaro cactus or what is referred to by biologists as the Arizona Upland subdivision of the Sonoran Desert (Fig. 12). The foothills and mountain ranges north of Phoenix and surrounding Tucson are well-known Gila monster haunts, and prime habitat can also be found near the towns of Safford, Superior, Florence, Gila Bend, Ajo, Wickenburg, Wikieup, and even Parker. The Papago (Tohono O'Odham) Indian reservation is almost entirely Gila monster country, as are large areas of Saguaro National Monument, Organpipe Cactus National Monument, and the Tonto National Forest. Much of the remaining Gila monster habitat is on desert lands administered by the Bureau of Land Management.

Figure 12. Gila monster habitat in Arizona -- Mazatzal Mountains. Note the abundance of boulders and mesquite trees.

Away from the paloverde-saguaro cactus plant community, Gila monsters become more sparse or localized and the chance of seeing one diminishes accordingly. And while the Gila monster is not uncommon in the semidesert grasslands of southeast Arizona, it is unusual to see one in the dry mountains of the southwestern part of the state and in most of the Mohave Desert of northwest Arizona. Gila monsters are decidedly rare in Grand Canyon National Park -- only four specimens had been reported as of 1980, and archaelogist Robert Euler has never seen one there in a decade of working in the Canyon. The same can also be said for the Kofa and Cabeza Prieta game ranges and on Lake Mead National Recreation Area. There are no Gila monsters in the Painted Desert and Navajo country of northern Arizona, and except for along the Colorado and Gila rivers, the animal appears to be absent from the extremely arid valleys of southwest Arizona.

New Mexico: As recently as the 1920's the occurrence of the Gila monster in the Land of Enchantment was a matter of debate. Since that time, however, dozens of these reptiles have been collected in southwest New Mexico in Hidalgo and Grant counties and the Gila monster's presence in this state has been definitely established. The vast majority of specimens come from along the Gila River near the Arizona border (Fig. 13) and the Peloncillo Mountains west of Lordsburg. Charles Painter, a herpetologist with the New Mexico Department of Game and Fish, states that, "the Gila monster is fairly common within their limited range in New Mexico," with that range extending as far north and east as near Silver City. Painter added that the Gila monster is sufficiently prevalent along the Gila River near Red Rock, New Mexico, that a research team plans to study the creature in that vicinity. Less certain are the origins of Gila monsters collected east of Deming in Luna County and in the vicinity of Kilbourne Hole west of Las Cruces in Doña Ana County. It is the opinion of Painter that these animals are probably released captives. The report of a Gila monster having been seen by members of the Wheeler Survey near San Ildefonso on the upper Rio Grande in August, 1874, is almost certainly in error, despite the statement that the "Pueblo Indians of this place said they were quite common."

Utah: Gila monsters in the Beehive State are confined to the southern half of Washington County in the state's extreme southwest corner. Here, the animal is further restricted to elevations below 3,200 feet in favorable habitats within the Mohave Desert. While not widely distributed, some good local populations are present, and two Gila monster studies have been conducted on Bureau of Land Management land in Paradise Canyon just northwest of Saint George. It is ironic that more has been learned about Gila monsters in this one part of Utah than in more representative habitats close to the animal's center of distribution in Arizona.

Nevada: Gila monsters have been known for some time to reside sparingly in Mohave Desert localities in southern Nevada, particularly in Clark County and extreme southern Lincoln county. More recent records place the lizards also in Red Rock Canyon (Fig. 14) and nearby canyons on the eastern slope of the Spring Mountain range northwest of Las Vegas.

California: Sightings of Gila monsters are so unusual in California that in 1949 a herpetologist from Indio published a paper challenging reports that the creature was native to the state, the author believing that Gila monster reports by miners and cowboys were cases of mistaken identity or releases. Indeed, as of 1982, only seven Gila monster records from five California locations had found their way into the scientific literature. All but one of these are from eastern San Bernardino County -- one on the west slopes of the Providence Mountains, one in the Clark Mountains, three from the Kingston Mountains, and one northwest of Needles in the Piute Mountains. The lone exception is one found on the California side of Imperial Dam on the Colorado River in Imperial County. With the exception of Imperial Dam, all of these locations are rather high in elevation (between 3,000 and 4,000 feet). One wonders if further investigations will reveal that Gila monsters also inhabit the Whipple, Chemehuevi, and Turtle mountains, as these ranges appear suitable for the animal.

Mexico: Gila monsters occur from the Arizona border southward through the Sonoran Desert to northwest Sinaloa. Southward from the vicinity of Alamos, Sonora, both species of Heloderms occur, the Gila monster favoring the more open thornscrub communites, and the Mexican beaded lizard being more common in the region's tropical deciduous forests (Map 1, Fig. 15). Gila monsters are also found in Sonora's higher foothills to an elevation of at least 3,500 feet, and although there are a number of records from Chihuahuan Desert and grassland areas in northeast Sonora, no specimen has yet been collected in the adjacent state of Chihuahua. The species is also apparently absent from Baja California, the Gran Desierto's arid sand dune region and Pinacate lava flow in northwest Sonora, and from the islands in the Gulf of California.

Figure 13. Gila monster habitat along the Gila River near Virden, New Mexico. Photo by M. H. Salmon.

Figure 14. Banded Gila monster habitat in Redrock Canyon, Nevada. As is the case farther south, boulders and shrubbery are important components of Gila monster habitat.

Figure 15. Reticulate Gila monster habitat north of Alamos, Sonora, Mexico. A few miles to the south the tropical vegetation becomes more dense and the Gila monster is replaced by the Mexican beaded lizard.

SUBSPECIES

Biologists recognize two subspecies or races of Gila monsters. The most common and well-known form is the Arizona or "reticulate" Gila monster (*Heloderma suspectum suspectum*), so named because the beaded pattern of the adults forms a network of irregular black blotches on a lighter background (reticulate means so marked as to form a network). Generally, the black covers a greater area than the orange or pink, and some individuals may be quite dark. This is especially so in the eastern portions of the lizard's range and among those animals dwelling among black lava rocks. The "type" specimen is the animal collected by Arthur Schott in 1855, appropriately, as it turns out, from near the center of the lizard's range -- the Sierra Morena on the Arizona-Sonora border. This race is characteristic of the Arizona Upland subdivision of the Sonoran Desert and adjacent habitats in Arizona, Sonora, and New Mexico (Map 2).

Gila monsters from western Arizona, Utah, Nevada, and California exhibit a definite banded or ringed pattern in which the orange or pink background usually covers a greater area than the black (Fig. 16, Map 2). This well-named "banded Gila monster" (*Heloderma suspectum cinctum*) is found in the Mohave Desert and the arid Lower Colorado River subdivision of the Sonoran Desert, the "type" specimen having been collected near Las Vegas, Nevada. Animals collected from the vicinity of Wickenburg, Arizona, and other locations near where the ranges of the two subspecies meet, display markings intermediate between the two types.

The banded Gila monster's retention of the ringed pattern found in all juvenile Gila monsters is interesting to taxonomists. Races of animals which retain their juvenile markings are considered to be closer to the ancestoral form than races which change their color markings as they grow older. If this assumption is true, the banded Gila monster is the more primitive of the two subspecies and closer to the parent stock than the reticulate subspecies which evolved to have a different adult color pattern. The retention of the juvenile markings in adults of the banded subspecies could also be interpreted to mean that this more northern race is closer to the species' place of origin than the reticulate Gila monster -- additional evidence of a northern origin for the lizard. No one of course *knows* why two different color patterns evolved, but some biologists believe that the more cryptic reticulate pattern evolved as the Gila monster moved southward into more diverse desertscrub and thornscrub habitats.

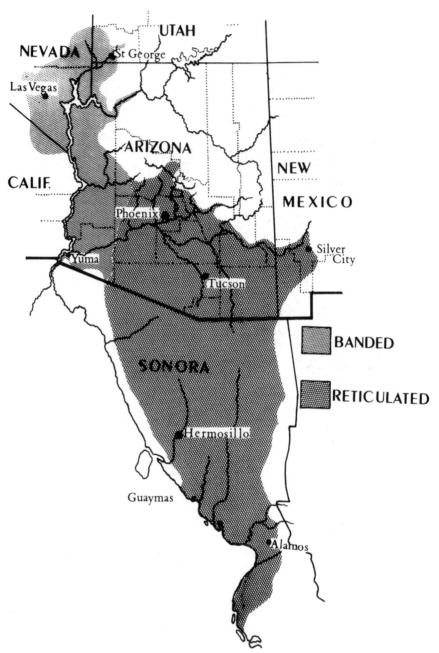

Map 2. Distributions of the reticulate and banded races of Gila monster.

Figure 16. Markings of a reticulate Gila monster (A) compared with a banded Gila monster (B).

VENOM

The deadly Gila monster is now the word. It has always been argued that this reptile did not bite and and that it was perfectly harmless. Some people have even gone so far to say that it was splendid eating when properly cooked, and that the Indians, especially, regarded it as a delicacy. It turns out now that the bite of the Gila monster is fatal.

Arizona Sentinel, (Yuma) October, 11, 1884

...exhaustive studies were made by some of the attachés of the Smithsonian Institution, among whom was Dr. R. W. Shufeldt, concerning the nature of the animal, and conclusions reached which the writer had previously attained -- that the reptile was non-venomous; and it may be accepted as conclusively demonstrated that the bite of the "monster" is innocuous *per se.*

George Goodfellow [M.D.], *Scientific American,* March 30, 1907.

Several early investigators, failing to recognize the venom glands, concluded that the Gila monster was non-poisonous, and that any symptoms of envenomation were really the result of infection from festering agents in the animal's saliva. For unlike poisonous snakes, whose venom is delivered through hollow hypodermic-like fangs from special glands behind the eyes in the upper jaws, the venom glands of the Gila monster are located beneath the skin toward the front of its lower jaw (Fig. 17). These glands have ducts that carry venom to mucous membranes between the lips of the lower jaw ending at a fold near the outer edge of the animal's lower teeth. This fold is thought to assist in the pumping of the poison along the grooves of the scimitar-shaped teeth when the animal clamps down and chews. The grooves are flanked by a sharp cutting edge that inflicts a puncture wound in front of the grooves, allowing the venom to flow readily into the wound by capillary action. The bite may be a brief nip or a vice-like grip that can be held for up to 15 minutes or so. Some venom is always released during the biting process but not all bites result in poison entering the wound. The longer the bite, the more venom is released.

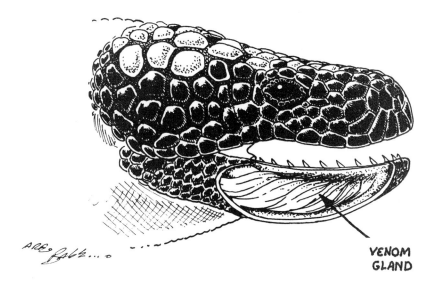

VENOM GLAND

Figure 17. Lower jaw of a Gila monster showing venom glands.

Besides inflicting severe pain, the venom causes a rapid drop in blood pressure that can induce hypotensive shock. In small warm-blooded animals the breathing quickens and then gradually ceases. Death results from respiratory failure, or from falling blood pressure, blood clotting, and cardiac arrest.

Much debate has centered on the potency and purpose of the venom. Although there is no question but that the poison kills small animals, it is rarely if ever fatal to large mammals, including man. Unlike that of poisonous snakes, the venom contains no anti-coagulants or digestive enzymes. Although the venom would help subdue a struggling victim, it is not needed to immobilize the Gila monster's usually defenseless prey, which commonly consists of juvenile rodents or baby birds, and the conventional wisdom is that the poison is a defense mechanism. The fact that the venom contains a substance producing instant and excruciating pain in humans certainly lends credence to such an explanation. Yet, to hold on to an assailant does not appear to be a good defensive technique. Rattlesnakes strike, inject their venom, and then quickly draw away, allowing their attacker to leave. The Gila monster hangs on to its assailant, yet does not kill a coyote or other large animal. Just how "teaching" an individual predator to leave a Gila monster alone helps prevent future attacks is unclear, but it makes sense that such a slow moving animal would have a defensive weapon to compensate for its inability to flee.

PHYSICAL ABILITIES

Not that the Gila monster is so very horrible, though he is as ugly as an ugly lizard can be, but he is accredited with so much power over everything with which he comes in contact -- so many stories are told of his certain death-dealing propensities, even his breath being accounted as fatal to life as that breathed forth by Rappacinni's daughter -- he is so invariably made the victor in contests with other reptiles, which all men shun, that his prowess, so far as newspaper fiction and the observation of zoological garden experts go to show, has come to be regarded as well nigh invincible. To add to the mysterious halo surrounding this ascribed power of dealing sure death in its most horrible form, he is credited with being himself invulnerable, short of anything less than the visitation of a landslide.

San Francisco Chronicle, ca. 1900

Vision, Hearing, and Agility: Gila monsters have good daytime vision and amazingly keen hearing, as anyone who has ever attempted to sneak up on a basking animal can attest. The animal can also sense an oncoming intruder by detecting minute vibrations in the ground -- a good thing given that the Gila monster is a slow traveler and incapable of high speed sprints. The average foraging mode is only 13 feet a minute or .15 miles per hour, with maximum bursts of about 50 feet per minute (one-half m.p.h.). But while the lizard does not move forward with speed, it is neither as awkward nor as sluggish as it first appears. The Gila monster can spin around and face an attacker with lightning suddenness. More than one handler of a Gila monster has been surprised by the animal's agility and quickness, particularly if one of the clawed feet obtains a grip on an article of clothing or other surface.

Strength and Tenacity: Popular accounts are rife with examples of the supposed power and endurance of the Gila monster. Fights have been staged between Gila monsters and a twelve-year-old alligator, a wildcat, a red coachwhip, a copperhead, and several varieties of rattlesnakes. In all of these accounts the Gila monster emerges triumphant, or at the very least, giving as good as he got. The only reptile known to best a Gila monster in combat is its ancient adversary, the desert tortoise. On two occasions, Bureau of Reclamation biologists observed female tortoises drive Gila monsters from the tortoise's nest site or burrow.

There is some justification for the animal's reputation as a combatant. Gila monsters are immune to their own poison and appear to be resistant to rattlesnake venom. Their hides are protected by a armor-like covering that only the sharpest and strongest of teeth can penetrate. Moreover, the Gila monster is capable of sustaining a higher level of activity for a longer period of time than any other lizard yet studied. One researcher, Dan Beck, observed thirteen different bouts between male Gila monsters, including a marathon three-hour battle which continued until dark. After circling one another, the two combatants shoved, grappled, bit, twisted and turned, each attempting to overturn its opponent. The bout ceased only when the loser rolled out from under the victor's straddle to make a hasty retreat. By the time the brawl ended the sun was down and the temperature of the winner had dropped from 92.5 degrees F. to 63 degrees F.

The Gila monster's tenacity of life is also legendary. Taxidermists and animal collectors have reported the lizard to be nearly indestructable, after attempting to club them to death, suffocate them, drown them, and even inject them with alcohol. Even today, rural residents of Sonora are said to assure the death of a Gila monster that they have killed by hanging it by the neck with a wire noose, lest the animal recover and seek vengence on its tormenter. This "refusal to die" is of course due to the reptile's low metabolic rate and primitive nervous system that allows the muscles to twitch long after the animal is clinically dead. The Gila monster, for all of its strength and endurance, is nonetheless a shy animal -- a fact known for some time:

> ...If escape be near in the shape of a burrow in the ground or
> a hole in the rocks large enough for its accommodation, the
> monster will discreetly retire from view and remain hidden
> until the enemy has retired.

> Frank Oakley, "Ugly as Sin Itself," *San Francisco
> Chronicle*, June 15, 1893

Digging, Climbing and Swimming:

> "I...became acquainted with...a feature so extraordinary, so
> altogether incredible that I almost hesitate to relate it,
> although I can produce to-day several witnesses who can and
> will swear to its truth. In order to preserve the skin without
> the least mutilation I thought that the best way to kill the

animal without much suffering was to drown it...I therefore attatched a heavy stone to the end of the wire around the animal's shoulders and immersed it in a barrel full of water, keeping the lizard completely under water, anchored as it were. But when I found after *twelve hours* of immersion that the Saurian was alive as ever, I bethought me of another manner of execution.

John Spring, "The Gila monster, a personal experience," 1889

As their powerful claws indicate, Gila monsters are prodigious diggers. That is how they make their living and seek shelter. The digging is all done with the forefeet, alternately scooping out earth or sand with successive strokes of the left and then right "hands." The motions are outward, not straight backwards like a dog's, the excavated material being thrown to the side and rear. While Gila monsters are undoubtedly capable of digging their own dens, they usually enlarge a natural crevice or a burrow already dug by some other animal. A Gila monster's den may reach a depth of three to five feet below the surface of the ground.

While primarily a terrestrial animal, the Gila monster is not adverse to climbing trees, shrubs, and even cholla cactus on occasion to search for bird nests. Gila monsters have been reported as "cautiously" climbing the trunks and stouter branches of mesquites, desert willows, and other rough-barked trees in Arizona and have been found as high as twenty-three feet above the ground in trees in Mexico. In returning from a climb, the lizard descends head-first like a squirrel, inching forward with its front feet, while anchoring itself with the hind feet. Both the chin and tail are used to control its descent. Gila monsters have also been observed climbing and descending nearly vertical cliff faces with little or no apparent difficulty.

Gila monsters are weak but persistent swimmers and take to the water without any hesitation. On entering the water, the limbs flail weakly along, the reptile propelling itself mostly by flexing the body and tail as if sculling. An interesting episode regarding the swimming ability of Gila monsters is related by Dr. W. L. Minckley, a zoology professor at Arizona State University. In March, 1974, Minckley observed the first filling of Painted Rock Reservoir on the Gila River southwest of Phoenix. Although the weather was cool and the water chilly, hundreds of snakes and numerous Gila monsters were attempting to escape the rising waters by swimming to the retreating shoreline or to the tops of inundated mesquite trees. According to Minckley, the Gila monsters gulped air to increase their bouancy and slowly but steadily paddled their way to shore where dozens of the animals were salvaged by biologists as specimens or for later release elsewhere.

Gila monsters appear to be almost incapable of drowning. A Phoenix undertaker reported many years ago that he "kept one under water for ten hours, taking him out at the end of that time still alive and in fighting condition." Another early experiment resulted in a Gila monster drowning in only three hours, but the lizard had been "hung up by the neck all the previous night." A more recent episode is reported by Terry Johnson (Nongame Branch Supervisor for the Arizona Game and Fish Department) who inadvertently left water dripping in a bathtub where he kept a Gila monster. On his return from a trip, a week later, the Gila monster was found floating atop the nearly overflowing tub, apparently none the worse for its prolonged aquatic experience. This amazing ability has been attributed to the lizard going into a state of suspended animation or torpor for hours at a time.

TEMPERATURE AND MOISTURE REGULATION

Rattlesnakes do not stay in the heat that the Gila monster enjoys, and it is doubtful if even a salamander could stand a daily temperature of 135 degrees for hours, which the Gila monster grows fat on during midsummer weeks.

Henry G. Tinsley, old newspaper clipping in the files of the Sharlot Hall Museum, Prescott, Arizona, ca. 1900

In reality, the Gila monster is less heat-tolerant and more cold-tolerant than most cold-blooded desert animals. Active Gila monsters have a low metabolism and a low body temperature in comparison with most other lizards. Readings from hundreds of Gila monsters in Utah and Arizona have shown that the animals normally maintain a body temperature from 75 degrees F. to 98 degrees F., with a preferred temperature range hovering between 82 and 85 degrees F.-- a relatively cool and narrow temperature range for a desert reptile. When the animal's temperature rises much above 92 degrees F., the lizard seeks cover in an attempt to lower its temperature to a more moderate level. Should the monster's temperature rise above 105 degrees F., its plight becomes critical and the animal is in danger of dying.

All this means that Gila monsters are normally active only when air temperatures are between about 67 and 99 degrees F., and when ground surface temperatures range from approximately 73 to 111 degrees F. To maintain a comfortable temperature in the mid-80's during the summer months, the lizard employs several strategies --

shuttling from sun to shade, carrying its body and tail above the ground, regulating its activity time, and spending considerable time underground.

Hibernating Gila monsters maintain body temperatures in the 50 degrees F. range when temperatures outside their shelters are well below freezing. Unlike other cold blooded reptiles, Gila monsters have been known to emerge from their winter dens and from their nighttime sleeping shelters when the temperature is as low as 55 degrees F. To achieve a more optimum temperature on cold days, the lizard will bask on a rock for several minutes to several hours in direct sunlight (Fig. 18). Gila monsters can also modify their temperatures by positioning themselves between boulders and seeking out other favorable microenvironments.

Gila monsters are said to have "leaky skins," and unlike other desert lizards, are in danger of drying out during the hot summer months. To maintain a healthy water balance, Gila monsters spend much of the summer in underground burrows where the humidity is higher and the temperature cooler than in the dry, hot air of the desert surface. Long periods of inactivity also retard water loss.

Figure 18. Basking Gila monster caught outside of its hibernaculum.

THE GILA MONSTER AT HOME

Habitat Requirements: Boulders and rough, rocky country are important components of Gila monster habitat, as these features provide most of the winter den sites or *hibernacula*. All of the 79 "shelters" found by researcher Dan Beck in Utah were in natural crevices under rocks, some of which had been modified by the lizard's digging. The entrance to a winter den usually has a southern exposure and the den itself may be deep underground and expansive. A choice *hibernaculum* may be used by the same Gila monster year after year and be shared with desert tortoises, rattlesnakes, and other lizards including another Gila monster.

Desert trees and shrubbery appear to be important constituents of Gila monster habitat. Not only do such plants as velvet mesquite trees, paloverde trees, triangle-leaf bursage, jojoba, and hackberry bushes provide shade and cover for the lizard, they are important habitat components for the lizard's prey. Dry washes or *arroyos* are especially favored by foraging Gila monsters as are mesquite thickets or *bosques* because these areas host the greatest numbers of nesting birds and cottontail rabbits. Flat plains, thinly populated by creosote bushes, are poor Gila monster country.

Burrows used in spring and summer differ from winter *hibernacula* in several respects. Summer shelters, which may be in rock crevices, tortoise "pallets" (dug earthen niches), packrat nests, or mammal burrows, are in essence, Gila monster "motels," used for resting, sleeping, and cooling down between forays. These summer shelters are usually no deeper than about three feet below the surface of the ground and are often under the shade of a tree or in dense vegetation to take advantage of the more moderate temperatures found there. Communal summer dens are not uncommon in prime habitat, and researchers have found as many as six Gila monsters using the same shelter.

Times of Active Behavior: It was not until after the development of miniaturized radio tracking equipment in the 1970's that researchers were able to follow Gila monsters on their travels. What they discovered was amazing. In two separate studies, biologists Lauren Porzer-Kepner and Dan Beck found that even when it is active less than five percent of the reptile's time is spent above ground! The creature comes out of its winter torpor in the spring to feed and mate, and resurfaces only irregularly thereafter. Gila monsters are only active for brief intervals during a 90-day peak activity period. Hence, more than 99 percent of the Gila monster's life is spent underground and out of sight.

Emergence from hibernation in spring is brought on by the onset of warm temperatures, and may be as early as late February or early March, depending on the weather and location. In southern Arizona the Gila monster's year usually begins about mid-March; farther north, it begins in late April. Springtime is also when the animals are out the most, and the vast majority of Gila monster activity occurs from mid-March through mid-June in Arizona, and between late April and early July in Utah and Nevada. Another, lesser flurry of activity takes place in southern Arizona and Sonora during the "monsoon" season from July through early September. May, however, is the "Gila monster month" throughout the animal's range and the time when most animals are seen by people. Although a few Gila monsters may be out as late as early November, progressively cooler temperatures put most of the animals in their winter quarters by October, and except to bask briefly in the sun on warm afternoons, they will not come out again until the following spring.

Temperatures also regulate daily activity patterns. During the cooler spring months the animals may be active throughout the morning and into the afternoon. Increasing temperatures and low humidity in June cause the Gila monster to seek cooler and moister surroundings underground and the animal aestivates or becomes summer-dormant. Those Gila monsters that do come out in summer do so primarily in the early morning or in the early evening. While not principally nocturnal creatures as is frequently stated, Gila monsters are sometimes seen out after dark once the summer rains begin in July, especially in the southern part of its range. By autumn, the reptiles are again found during the middle of the day, but not as commonly as in spring.

By spending most of its time resting and sleeping, the Gila monster expends less energy than other reptiles including many so-called "sit-and-wait" lizards which depend on prey coming to them. This less than energetic life-style does not mean that the Gila monster is lazy as some popular writers have described him. It only signifies that the animal's energy requirements are such that it doesn't need to hunt more often.

Movements and Home Ranges: On emerging from its torpor in the spring, the Gila monster may make several erratic forays in the vicinity of its hibernaculum or winter den. As the days warm up, the lizard then generally moves down slope in search of food and a mate, usually working its way along an *arroyo* or following a *bajada* (foothill slope) to a valley location. There appears to be no difference in the time of emergence for males and females.

Daily movements may consist of a brief forage around a temporary shelter or be a more lengthy expedition of up to half a mile. Dan Beck found that an average sortie for a Gila monster in Utah lasted for a little under an hour and covered about 700 feet. Over a period of several days, adult males may travel a mile or more in their search for food and mates. Females are more sedentary

Seasonal movements may be impressive. Over one spring and summer, eight Gila monsters near Queen Creek, Arizona, ranged from less than 0.5 mile to more than 2.5 miles. Three marked Gila monsters in southwestern Utah traveled distances ranging from 0.8 miles to 2.2 miles on their spring forays. One male was calculated to have covered a distance of nearly 6.5 miles over a year's time.

By following lizards with radio transmitters, Lauren Porzer-Kepner determined that the minimum home range of Gila monsters in the Queen Creek area ranged from about 30 acres to nearly 70 acres and averaged around 40 acres. Most of the home ranges tended to be longer than wide. Gila monsters at the periphery of the animal's distribution in Utah had larger home ranges with two males covering an average area of around 120 acres. The one female monitored only had a home range of 14 acres. Several home ranges overlapped those of other Gila monsters, and except for breeding males fighting for dominance, these generally solitary creatures appear to be relatively tolerant of their neighbors.

FOOD HABITS

A Gila Monster was brought to town Thursday afternoon and amused a number of people on Broad Street. He was a lively cuss, and struck viciously at everyone who approached him. In speaking of their vitality and of the great length of time that they can live without food, Dr. Pangburn of San Carlos, mentioned having kept one in a box for seven months without food and it was apparently as healthy and lively at the end of that time as when captured.

Arizona Silver Belt (Globe), April 25, 1885

Gila monsters are opportunistic foragers; that is, they actively hunt and seek whatever foods are available. By necessity, these slow-moving carnivores feed primarily on defenseless baby animals and eggs which they detect and identify through chemical cues and odors picked up by their constantly flicking snake-like tongues. Unlike other lizards, which hunt by sight, the Gila monster's tongue transmits the odor of hidden prey to a special scent organ in the roof of the mouth called the Jacobson's organ. The kind of prey taken depends on the time of year and location, but is known to include baby desert cottontails, baby antelope and round-tailed ground squirrels, and the helpless young of other rodents found in underground nests. Gambel's quail eggs, desert tortoise and other reptile eggs, and the eggs and nestlings of doves and other birds are also sometimes eaten, along with what lizards the monster can corner. The number of observations of feeding Gila monsters in the wild are few, and other items such as subterranean insect larvae may possibly also be consumed on occasion.

Eggs are swallowed whole if not too large, or broken and the contents lapped up along with quantities of sand and grit. Baby rabbits and fledgling birds are repeatedly bitten and worked about until their head is in the monster's mouth. The entire victim is then gulped down in stages, the Gila monster standing rigidly on his forefeet, head held high in the air (Fig. 19). While the swallowing of a baby bird or mammal may take a long time, there is no chewing to indicate that the prey is being purposely envenomated more than what would normally occur through natural salivary action.

The activity pattern of the Gila monster is superbly adapted to take advantage of what prey might be available: Gambel's quail nest in April and May, the peak number of desert cottontail births is also in April and early May, and the height of the mourning and white-winged dove nesting season is in May. Another, smaller reproductive surge occurs for cottontails and doves shortly after the onset of the summer rains in July in southern Arizona and Sonora. Desert tortoises lay eggs from May through early August. Taking advantage of these sequences, the Gila monster tends to work washes and north slopes for quail nests early in the season and forages for rabbit and rodent nests in flatter terrain later in the year. One has to wonder what happens to Gila monsters during those springs following an unusually dry winter when few quail nest and the number of young cottontails is almost nil.

Although every egg in a nest may not always be consumed, the usual situation is for the lizard to eat the entire clutch of eggs or as many nestling animals as are available. The amount of food eaten at one time may therefore be large, and young Gila monsters have been known to ingest up to one-half of their weight at one time. As a result, relatively few meals are needed, and it has been estimated that the eggs in three quail nests provide all the rations an adult male Gila monster needs to survive until the following year. The animal's large size, low resting metabolism, and long periods of inactivity simply make more frequent feeding unnecessary. Cold-blooded reptiles need only a small percentage of the calories required by warm-blooded animals of similar size.

The Gila monster's tail is a good indicator of its physical condition. A plump, well-rounded tail is the trademark of a well-fed, healthy animal; a skinny triangular-shaped tail indicates the Gila monster is starving and dehydrated. Serving as a fat storage-locker, the Gila monster's tail is not detachable as is the tail of many other species of lizards.

Figure 19. Characteristic pose of a feeding Gila monster in the process of swallowing a woodrat. Photo by Randy Babb.

The prey provides the Gila monster not only with food but is the lizard's source of water. While Gila monsters readily drink water when it is provided, they do not go to water like some desert animals. Nor is water usually available to them under natural conditions; May and June are normally the driest months in the Sonoran, Chihuahuan, and Mohave deserts.

The growth rate of wild adult Gila monsters is slow and averages only from one-tenth to one-fifth of an inch a year, depending on the animal's size and condition. Even well fed captives only grow about two-fifths of an inch in a year's time. Weight gains, though, may be impressive. One male increased its fall weight of 25 1/2 ounces to 31 ounces by eating one young cottontail the following spring -- a weight increase of more than 20 percent. Young Gila monsters grow at a faster rate than the adults, and hatchlings may grow two inches or more a year in the first three years or so.

SEX LIFE, REPRODUCTION, AND SOCIABILITY

The Gila monster was formerly common in the Gila river and neighboring streams. But the species is already rare, and is rapidly becoming extinct. It exterminates itself, because the creatures have the habit of eating their own eggs. Curious, isn't it? When the Gila monsters eat their eggs they never hatch [lay] any more.

Old newspaper clipping in the files of the Sharlot Hall Museum, Prescott, Arizona, ca. 1900

With the approach of the breeding season, soon after the Gila monsters emerge from their hibernacula, the adult males, tolerant of each other's presence at other times of the year, become aggressive. Scent marks are made by rubbing the vent on rocks or other objects as the search for a female begins. Competing males engage in vicious fights that may last from a few minutes to several hours before the loser becomes exhausted and leaves the battlefield. Victory invariably goes to the larger and stronger lizard.

Should a female be encountered, a wonderful courtship ritual involving much tongue-caressing, chin-rubbing, and nose-nudging begins. The actual mating involves a side-to-side embrace in which the male's head is atop the female's neck, with one rear leg over her pelvic area and the corresponding foreleg over her shoulder. Insertion of one or the other lobe of the male's twin-pronged hemipenis is assisted by the female raising her tail and gaping her vent. Copulation lasts from several minutes to several hours and may continue until after dark.

After a gestation period of about 45 days, a clutch of from two to 12, but more commonly about five, leathery elongate-shaped eggs are laid in July or August. Each egg is about two and one-half inches long and one and one-fourth inches in diameter and weighs around one and one-third ounces (Fig. 20). No biologist has yet discovered a Gila monster nest in the wild so the animal's natural egg-laying locations and procedures remain a mystery. Although a turn-of-the-century reptile collector named Ralston claimed to have found several nests and to have observed a female scooping out a hole in moist sand from three to five inches deep in which to lay her eggs, the details of his description make his story highly suspicious.

Figure 20. Gila monster emerging from egg. Photo by Howard Lawler, Arizona-Sonora Desert Museum.

Nor has anyone ever witnessed Gila monsters hatching under natural conditions. Nonetheless, sightings of juvenile monsters weighing only a few ounces between late April and early June indicate that hatching occurs the spring following mating and egg-laying. This suggests an unusually long ten-month incubation period, or an entire year from mating to hatching. Such is not the case with captive Gila monsters which may breed and hatch at odd times under artificial conditions. Eggs laid by captive Gila monsters in summer and incubated in controlled laboratory environments take from 128 to 135 days to hatch, so that the baby Gila monsters arrive in late November or December. Because hatchlings do not emerge in nature in mid-winter, herpetologists believe that either the embryonic development is prolonged in wild Gila monsters, or that the hatchlings remain in the nest until spring. But until a natural nest is found and monitored, just what happens is another Gila monster secret.

Baby Gila monsters come into the world looking much like the adults and with fully developed teeth and venom glands. The only major difference between them and the adults is the youngster's small size and pale cream coloration between distinct dark bands. Six to eight weeks after emerging from the egg, laboratory hatchlings began taking on the colors and markings of the adults.

ENEMIES, MORTALITY, AND LONGEVITY

One physical peculiarity of the monster is shown by the fact that a fifty-pound boulder dropped upon its back is not liable to kill it, but a slight blow on the side of the head with a walking stick produces instant death.

Arizona Graphic, September 23, 1899

Man appears to be the Gila monster's only serious enemy. Dogs may occasionally attack one, but the results are rarely fatal or even damaging to the Gila monster. The only written account of an animal preying upon one of these lizards is the reported recovery of a 16-inch Gila monster from the stomach of a 40-inch black-tailed rattlesnake. Since the snake had no visible injuries, it is possible that the monster had been weakend or was nearly dead before being swallowed.

Several wild mammals, including coyotes, foxes, badgers, skunks, bobcats, and mountain lions have been suggested as possibly preying on Gila monsters. But Dr. Norm Smith at the University of Arizona, who supervised coyote studies in prime Gila monster country south of Tucson, found no instance of Gila monster remains in an extensive collection of coyote scats. Similarly, Dr. Robert Ohmart at Arizona State University stated that he did not know of any Gila monster parts in kit fox droppings in an area near Queen Creek, Arizona, where both species were studied. The only known occurrences of this lizard in mammal droppings are remnants of Gila monsters in three mountain lion scats collected over several years in the desert west of Wickenburg by researcher Jenny Cashman.

Of the potential avian predators, those most likely to feed on Gila monsters are the Harris hawk and red-tailed hawk. Jim Dawson, who studied Harris hawks in Arizona for more than ten years, and who is the recognized authority on this raptor, has never found Gila monster remains in the thousands of hawk nests that he has examined for prey items fed to nesting females and young. Despite his study area being in excellent Gila monster habitat, and the Harris hawk's two nesting seasons coinciding with the Gila monster's peak activity periods, Dawson only found the remains of birds, mammals, and other species of lizards in the nests. At our request, Dawson checked with another researcher who had investigated the food habits of red-tailed hawks in the Sonoran Desert. While numerous snakes, including rattlers, have been recorded as red-tailed hawk food items, no incidence of this hawk feeding on Gila monsters was reported. It therefore appears that at least adult Gila monsters are without a serious natural predator.

As befits a carnivorous animal at the top of the food chain, the Gila monster has a low natural mortality and a population of these lizards needs to produce only a few young each year to maintain its numbers. Gila monsters in captivity can live for 20 to 30 years and it may be assumed that wild animals are also long-lived. The main cause of death for Gila monsters at present appears to be road-kills on highways and from surprise altercations with ignorant or mean-spirited humans. More importantly, a significant but unknown number of Gila monsters are removed from the wild population each year as captives or because they are considered unwanted neighbors.

There is no question but that the Gila monster is under seige. Hundreds of square miles of Gila monster habitat have been lost in the clearing of mesquite forests and desert for agriculture during the last one hundred years. Highways take an increasing toll of these lizards and new roads continue to isolate formerly continuous populations. Concrete-lined canals are barriers to the movement of Gila monsters and fracture their home ranges. Most detrimental of all, has been the unrelenting expansion of cities and urban developments into formerly remote Gila monster habitat. Here, even those lizards that escape the destruction of their habitat by the initial construction activities are eventually doomed to be trapped in swimming pools, run over on streets, or simply removed as creatures incompatible with human occupation. Fortunately, sizable areas of Gila monster country are protected from development in national parks and monuments and in federal wilderness areas.

POPULATION STATUS

Now to this day, many people think there is no such thing as the Gila monster. And yet, throughout the Colorado desert, especially along the Gila river, you may encounter thousands...

Professor Myron P. Kirk of the Smithsonian Institution, old newspaper article on file at the Sharlot Hall Museum, Prescott, Arizona. ca. 1900

No method of counting Gila monsters has been devised so there is no way of knowing how many there are or whether the animals are increasing or decreasing. Nonetheless, some of the old accounts make one wonder if the animal has not decreased in numbers. While conducting a Gambel's quail study on the Santa Rita Experimental Range south of Tucson in the early 1930's, David M. Gorsuch found 37 Gila monsters during two quail nesting seasons. Could he have found as many Gila monsters there today? Until a census method is devised and population studies are conducted, about all that can be said is that the Gila monster is an unevenly distributed animal, relatively common in certain habitats, but rare or absent in others. But even where it is most abundant it is rarely seen. This propensity to remain hidden is its best defense and its salvation. The Gila monster is not yet an endangered species but wilderness protection of its desert home is essential to insure the Aztec lizard's continued American presence.

PART II HUMANS AND GILA MONSTERS

THE GILA MONSTER IN INDIAN CULTURES

The Pima, Apache, Maricopah and Yuma Indians of the Southwest, who have little fear of the bite of a Mexican centipede or a rattlesnake, will hunt a Gila monster cautiously to its death, and even go many miles to rid the country of one of these reptiles, which they regard as the most to be dreaded of anything that crawls. Among the Cocopahs of Lower California the tribal belief is that the most fearful vengence that may come to the spirit bodies of bad Indians after this life, is to be bitten by a red Gila monster that roams, unseen by mortal eyes, over the adobe plains waiting to snap at the red-skinned savages inimical to the great spirit chief.

H. G. Tinsley, newspaper clipping at the Sharlot Hall Museum, Prescott, Arizona, ca. 1900

Regardless of how unusual the Gila monster appears to us, the Gila monster did not play an especially prominent role in Southwest Indian cultures. The reptile's confinement to the Sonoran Desert and its environs brought the animal in contact primarily only with the Tohono O'Odham (Papago), Pima, Seri, Colorado River Indians, and certain Apache tribes. Among these people the Gila monster was regarded as a normal neighbor and not as an especially bizarre or extraordinary creature. We know of no Gila monster clans or totems.

Nor is there any evidence to suggest any consumptive uses of the Gila monster by native Americans despite an October 11, 1884, account in a Yuma newspaper, the *Arizona Sentinel*, claiming that the reptile "was splendid eating when properly cooked, and that the Indians, especially, regarded it as a delicacy." A probably more accurate statement was made by Frank Oakley of Tucson and printed in the June 15, 1893, issue of the *San Francisco Chronicle*: "As for Apaches, it is well known that they hate fish and reptiles of all kinds and never eat them [Gila monsters] even if starving to death."

Gila Monsters and Disease: Although U. S. Army officer Charles Bendire observed that the "Apache Indians believe that the very breath of this lizard could cause death," Southwestern Indians were cautious around Gila monsters for reasons other than their poisonous properties. The Tohono O'Odham and Pimas, closely related peoples, had a healthy respect for most animals, believing them to possess a spiritual power

49

capable of causing sickness if a person killed, touched, or looked at them in an improper manner. As such, animals were capable of great mischief, and the ailments they produced were more feared than the animal itself.

The Tohono O'Odham, who call the Gila monster *cheadagi*, believed that the lizard was particularly dangerous if stepped on or if a nursing mother crossed its path. According to anthropologist Ruth Underhill, the Tohono O'Odham believed that the result of such an encounter would be sore feet, or if the animal was actually stepped on, sores all over the body. Nursing mothers might lose their milk. The prescribed remedy was to catch the Gila monster, tie a red rag around its neck, and send it on its way taking the evil with it. A fetish or an effigy carved from a saguaro rib and festooned with a red rag could be substitued if the actual animal was no longer available. A remedial song could also be sung by a shaman:

> *A lizard maiden*
> *Was thirsty and crying.*
> *A gila monster ran up*
> *And was comforting her.*
> *The lizard stopped, and then*
> *The gila monster carried her off*
> *And took her to wife.*

or:

> *Down I sit;*
> *Songs I begin.*
> *Down I sit;*
> *Songs I begin.*
> *Here around me*
> *All the earth shakes.*

Anthropologist Frank Russell found that the Pimas held similar beliefs, and thought that if a prospective father killed a Gila monster just before the birth of his child, the baby's body could become red and feverish. Again, the remedy for such a rare occurrence was to sing the "Gila monster song" four times:

> *Pitiable harlot though I am,*
> *My heart glows with the singing*
> *While the evening yet is young.*
> *My heart glows with the singing.*

Legends and Myths: The Tohono O'Odham Indians have a charming legend to explain the origin of the Gila monster's brightly-colored and oddly-textured skin. One of several tales collected in the 1920's by novelist Harold Bell Wright, the story describes the first saguaro wine festival held centuries ago. Not only did the Indians participate, but all of the animals were invited. Naturally, everyone wanted to look his best for the feast so they donned their most handsome garb. To enhance his appearance, the Gila monster gathered bright pebbles and made himself a coat that was as durable as it was beautiful -- a covering which he wears to this day.

The Chemehuevis, a small tribe along the lower Colorado River, also had a legend regarding the Gila monster which was fortunately recorded in the delightful book *The Chemehuevis* by Carobeth Laird, an Anglo woman married to a Chemehuevi man. This epic saga tells of a conflict between two groups, Coyote and his followers, and the rock-shirted Gila monster and Turtle (Desert Tortoise) and their band. As in other Chemehuevi myths, the characters are not really animals displaying animal-like behaviors, but stand-ins for people -- the Chemehuevis. The story relates "How Coyote went to war against Gila Monster," and as is often the case in southwestern Indian mythology, the tricky Coyote eventually comes out on top:

> Gila Monster and Turtle were companions and partners. Both were chiefs. Gila Monster was the High Chief, and Turtle was the lesser chief. Those two were the heads of a very large band. Gila Monster and Turtle instructed their people well. When a good year came, the women gathered seeds and stored them in large baskets capped with potsherds and sealed with greasewood gum. They gathered fruit and berries, which they dried and stored. They boiled the heart of mescal plants and pounded them out into slabs two or three feet across. The hunters brought in much meat. Some of it was pounded and dried, like the mescal hearts, and some was made into jerky. Then the people dug a big hole and buried all the food they had prepared.
>
> They covered it well and made the surface of the ground look like it had not been disturbed. Afterwards the whole band went to roam around the country. Because it was such a good year, they could find food everywhere and could travel wherever they pleased. There came a bad year. Coyote and his people were living near the place where Gila Monster and his people had stored their food, but because it was so well hidden, they did not know about it. Coyote had not told his people to prepare food and store it, and the result was that they now had nothing at all to eat. Coyote wandered off alone to see if he could find anything. He saw one solitary bean on a screw mesquite tree. He shot it down with an arrow, and the

51

bean dropped into a little hole in the ground. Coyote went over to dig it out, but the more he dug, the further the bean rolled down along a crack in the dry earth. The bean kept rolling, and Coyote kept digging, till at last he uncovered the food the people of Gila Monster had buried. "I have good luck," he shouted, "I have found much food!"

Coyote made his home right there. He did not go back and tell his starving people about the food. He just stayed there, eating his way deeper and deeper into the hole.

In the meantime, Gila Monster and Turtle had said to their people, "We are having a bad year. Let us return to our food cache." Then they started home. As they approached the place where the food had been stored, Coyote heard voices. He looked out of the hole and saw many people coming. They were already very near. By this time Coyote had eaten almost all the food in the cache.

Coyote was frightened. "My penis, what shall I do?" he cried.

His penis advised him, "Make yourself dead. Make yourself into a coyote carcass."

Coyote became an old, dead coyote, one that looked as if it had been lying there for several months. The people of Gila Monster and Turtle said, "This is the place all right - but look! Just look what that coyote has done to our food! And there he lies dead! He smells bad - somebody take a stick and throw him out!"

Two men took a long stick, worked it under the carcass, and tossed the stinking thing out of the hole. Coyote hit the ground alive and running, and with a good headstart. He called back over his shoulder, taunting the people he had wronged, "How could you know that I was fooling you?"

The people were terribly angry. They followed Coyote in hot pursuit. As he reached his own camp he called out, "Prepare for war! Prepare for war! Gila Monster is on the warpath! His people are coming after us!"

Gila Monster and Turtle with all their warriors were right on his heels. Coyote's people were unprepared and weak from hunger. Almost all of them were killed or taken captive. When Coyote saw that his side was losing, he ran away and hid himself, and some of his people went with him.

Later, in a continuation of the saga, one of Coyote's descendants divides himself into two doves called Dove Boys (mourning and white-winged doves?). Together, and with the help of other animals, they lead Coyote's people on a mission of revenge against Gila Monster and

Turtle. After a series of ruses, the suspicious Gila Monster falls to subterfuge and is killed along with Turtle by Coyote's warriors.

Unlike the Tohono O'Odham, the Seri Indians, who live on the Sonora coast, do not view the Gila monster as a source of disease but as medicine. According to linguist Mary Beck Moser, the Seris believe that the skin of a Gila monster, when heated and placed on the forehead, cures a headache. In the old days the Seris would sometimes wear sections of the skin of a Gila monster's tail as decorative finger rings.

The Yaqui Indians of Sonora also believed in the healing powers of the Gila monster's hide. Their *curanderos* (healers) would place the skin of a Gila monster over a person's diseased or infected parts in the belief that the poison would be removed, allowing the patient's wound to heal.

According to a number of early accounts, some Indians thought that Gila monsters could control the weather by talking directly to the Storm Spirit. The Apaches were also said to consider the presence of a Gila monster as a sign of imminent rain. The primary involvement of Indians with Gila monsters after American settlement, however, was to capture them for sale to the newcomers:

> In southern Arizona [Phoenix] many years ago two young fellows started a curio store -- one of the earliest of its kind...Our collection of wild things grew amazingly. The word spread over the Indian reservations like wild fire, and every Apache, Pima, Papago, Maricopa and Yuma Indian in that region devoted his energies to the capture of some wild animal, bird, or creeping thing to turn into two-bit pieces at our curio store...I have understood that Arizona stands at the head of the list in the wide variety of its snake population. Well, we had 'em all, and then some...Add to this Gila monsters, chuck-awallas...and lizards without end...We built pens and cages galore, and then enlarged them within a week to make room for new arrivals. Finally, through judicious advertising in eastern and foreign papers, we found a ready market for rattlers and certain other snakes, together with the Gila Monsters...

> Will C. Barnes, "An Arizona Snake Story," *Arizona Silver Belt* (Miami), March 28, 1924

The Gila Monster in Indian Art: Pictographs and designs of lizards that appear to be Gila monsters are not uncommon in the art of the Tohono O'Odham and Pima's predecessors, the Hohokam. A bowl at the Arizona State Museum from Snaketown, depicted in the May 1967 issue of *National Geographic*, is adorned with three fully formed figures that are good replicas of Gila monsters. Gila monster-like effigies have also been uncovered, not all of which found their way into museum collections:

> Mr. H. R. Patrick has a curious relic hung to his watch chain. It seems to represent a Gila Monster, and is cut out of a sea shell. He dug it up in the ruins east of town.

> *Phoenix Herald*, August 6, 1883

Pima and Tohono O'Odham baskets adorned with Gila monster designs may be seen at the Heard Museum in Phoenix, the Gila River Community Museum near Casa Blanca, and the city of Gila Bend's historical society museum (Fig. 21). Curators at these institutions state that these baskets were made between 1912 and 1935. Since traditional basket designs were limited to geometric patterns, it is clear that these baskets were intended by their makers for sale to Anglo buyers who must have appeared to the Indians to have been inordinately fascinated by these reptiles.

Figure 21. Pima Indian depiction of Gila monsters and swastikas on a woven basket at the Gila River Indian Community Museum, ca. 1930.

In southwest New Mexico, the Gila monster was an inspiration for the art of another ancient tribe. The Mimbres were a communal people who established villages from the Mimbres River Valley, the center of their culture, west to the edge of what is now southeast Arizona. From about 900 to 1100 A.D., they produced hand painted designs on pottery that are generally considered to be unrivalled for beauty and creativity among those produced by any other prehistoric native Americans. Along with the jackrabbit and the Gambel's quail, lizards resembling the Gila monster were among the most commonly depicted of nature's creatures on Mimbres painted bowls. Not surprisingly, modern artists have cashed-in on the quality and popularity of the Mimbres designs, and the Mimbres style of Gila monster may now be found on hat pins, belt buckles, coffee cups and cereal bowls.

EARLY ACCOUNTS BY WESTERN MAN

Accounts of life in eighteenth century Sonora by two European priests make it clear that the natives were well aware of the *escorpión*'s poisonous nature. Its venom was said to be terrible, and according to Father Ignaz Pfefferkorn, "there is believed to be no remedy in the world for it, and it is said that he who is thus poisoned will be a corpse in a few hours." Another friar, Juan Nentvig, claimed that the thing to do if bitten was to cut away the affected parts immediately. He then went on to repeat some of the then prevailing wisdom about the Gila monster: "It runs very rapidly after its prey and seems to draw its victim to it with its deadly breath..."

The earliest account that we have found of Anglo-Americans coming upon a Gila monster described an incident that occurred in 1854. A group of Texas cowboys were trail-herding cattle across southern Arizona, bound for beef-scarce California, when they encountered an unusual beast about 30 miles northwest of the village of Tucson. One of the drovers, James G. Bell, kept a diary during the journey, and his entry for September 26 reads:

> Some of the men brought an animal into camp which is rather a curiosity; its body is covered with rings of yellow and brown scales, short and fleshy tail, strong legs with five sharp exposed claws like a cat's, large blunt mouth with sharp teeth and no fangs...it is about fourteen inches long.

The next American to record discovering a Gila monster was artist and naturalist Arthur Schott who collected the animal in 1855 that was eventually to become the type specimen described by Edward Cope.

Schott was a member of the team surveying the new boundary between Arizona and Sonora created by the Gadsden Purchase and acquired his specimen in the Sierra Morena, a small mountain range straddling the international border at the southern boundary of the Papago Indian Reservation.

Three years later, in 1858, pioneer mining man Samuel P. Heintzelman reported stumbling upon a Gila monster near his mine in the Cerro Colorado Mountains about 30 miles southwest of Tucson. While resting in a dismal adobe hovel in the Old Pueblo, then a village of about 600 souls, Heintzelman wrote:

> We yesterday met on the road what the Mexicans call an *Escopión* or spitter. They have wonderful tales of its poison. This specimen was about 18 inches long, with legs and tail resembling a lizard but the ugliest reptile I ever saw. It is covered with what appears to be bead work, in yellow and black figures. I killed it, put a noose around its neck and brought it in.

Dr. B. I. D. Irwin was an army surgeon with a naturalist's bent stationed in southern Arizona during the 1850's and 1860's. In February, 1859, he wrote a report to his superiors detailing conditions at and near Fort Buchanan southeast of Tucson. Irwin discussed the flora and fauna of the region, including the animal we now know as the Gila monster:

> The "escupion" or spitter is a large variety of lizard, from twelve to twenty-four inches long, eight inches in circumference, beautifully marked with black and lemon-colored elevated spots, slow in its movements, and making a hissing noise when irritated, and thrusting its tongue from its mouth after the manner of a serpent. By the Mexicans and Indians it is reputed to be deadly poisonous; so much so that they never attempt to kill it, lest, during the act, the animal might spit on them, which they consider sufficient to cause a speedy death. I have every reason to doubt the truth of their belief, and presume that the ugly appearance of the creature has given to it its bad character. Those that I have taken alive showed no disposition to injure.

As the above accounts indicate, the term Gila monster was not yet in use in the late 1850's and the animal was referred to by its Mexican name. It is a bit odd that all these reporters describe the lizards as being yellow or lemon-colored and black, whereas most specimens from southern Arizona seen today tend to be more of an orange and black.

56

Ornithologist and army surgeon Elliott Coues was stationed at Fort Whipple near Prescott, Arizona, from July, 1864, to October, 1865. Much of his time was spent collecting specimens of various vertebrate animals, including reptiles, and sending them to the National Museum in Washington. In 1875, Dr. Coues published a paper on the reptiles and batrachians (frogs and toads) of Arizona based on his experiences and collections acquired a decade earlier. While in Arizona Territory, he obtained only one Gila monster:

> The specimen was taken in the desert in the vicinity of La Paz on the Colorado River [about 150 miles upstream from Fort Yuma], and I am confident it does not occur in the higher mountainous parts of the Territory. The "Gila Monster," as this large and repulsive looking reptile is called, appears to be not uncommon in the hot, southern parts of the Territory. A poisonous property is attributed to its saliva by the Mexicans, with whom the belief is also prevalent that it has the power of spirting its supposed venom.

The earliest mention of Gila monsters that we have found in a newspaper published within the area occupied by the lizard appeared in the *Arizona Citizen* (Tucson) on September 9, 1876:

> Some boys caught a Gila monster on Thursday, which is about eighteen inches in length. It is regarded as unusually large. H. Buehman, photographer, has it in alcohol.

As the decade of the 1870's drew to a close, the human population of the Southwest was rapidly expanding. Incidents involving Gila monsters began to be reported with increasing frequency in the growing numbers of newspapers and magazines published in the region. As the number of new citizens grew, so did the Gila monster's reputation, and old and new tales regarding this amazing lizard's properties proliferated.

MEXICAN AND AMERICAN FOLKLORE

> A few years ago the following well-authenticated fact occurred in the Huachuca Mtns. A wood cutter who had lay down in complete health to sleep wrapped up in his blanket, failed to arise in the morning when his co-laborers called him. Upon uncovering him, they found him stone dead, and near his body a Gila monster, which, in the bustle and confusion of the moment made good his escape. As the body of the man

bore no marks of a bite or other wounds, we must suppose that his death was caused by the mere exhalation of the lizard.

Arizona Citizen (Tucson), May 15, 1890

Fantastic Fables: The belief by Mexicans that the Gila monster's breath was poisonous, and their stories of *escorpiónes* blowing poisonous vapors containing droplets of deadly saliva were readily accepted by gullible Americans and embellished by imaginative journalists. "Eyewitness" accounts tell of monsters exhaling puffs of black vapor, fogging the air with a poisonous, white frothy spray, and:

> When bending over the reptile to cut off its head, the creature blew its breath in his face and he was instantly nauseated. A brother officer received the "monster's" breath full in the face and was at once nauseated and fell over on his back completely prostrated...

> Statement attributed to Dr. E. A. Mearns by M.Y.B. in "The Gila Monster," *Scientific American*, August 25, 1894.

An 1890 article in the *Scientific American* gives a practical, if fictitious, reason for such antics:

> "[The Gila monster]...emits its breath in a series of quick gasps. The breath is very fetid and its odor can be detected at some little distance from the lizard. It is supposed that this is one way in which the monster catches the insects and small animals which form a part of its food supply -- the foul gas overcoming them.

The belief that the Gila monster's breath was both poisonous and nauseous persisted into recent times:

> I once kept a cage of Gila Monsters for observation and study. I dissected and examined the teeth and other parts of the body under a magnifying glass. I found no venom except a gaseous form of poison, apparently produced by the eating of a carrion. This poison gas is exhaled as a means of defense and is offensive and sickening.

> J. W. Aker, "The Gila Monster," *Arizona Times* (Phoenix), March 12, 1949

Besides a mistaken assumption that the creature was especially fond of carrion and overripe eggs, many thought that this deadly halitosis was due to the accumulation of waste products caused by the Gila monster's lack of an anus. This belief in a missing orifice was common through the 1930's, despite numerous articles disavowing such a unique form of autointoxication. Again, the *Scientific American* speculated on the real reason for the Gila monster being a walking septic tank. This time in a 1907 article by "M":

> Old settlers here know of many cases of Gila monster poisoning, in which the effect was death. I believe that the bite of the Gila monster is dangerous because of the creature's habit of eating lizards, bugs, and rodents, and then lying on the sand so hot that it blisters the hands and feet. The heat causes the food to putrefy in the stomach, evidenced by the fact that the teeth are often covered with a fermented, putrefied froth from the food. A bite has the same effect as the cut of a dissecting knife used on a cadaver, in other words, the inoculation of a deadly poison.

So malodorous was the Gila monster from its lack of a conventional waste disposal system that:

> When the body is opened up a strong and disagreeable odor fills the room. This odor clings for days to objects coming in contact with any of the fluids from the body. One fair whiff of the monster's breath will turn an ordinary stomach.
>
> Ernest Douglas, "The Gila Monster, a Convicted Suspect," 1910

While such tales are patently untrue or gross exaggerations, like many legends, they do have some basis in fact. The venom of an agitated Gila monster does have a faintly sweet though not disagreeable odor. Like other animals, frightened Gila monsters may also sometimes regurgitate a recent meal when molested. Such partially-digested stomach contents may well have an offensive air to them. It is also not unreasonable to assume that droplets of saliva may occasionally be expelled when the animal hisses. Gila monsters also possess paired scent glands in the anal opening which are presumably used to announce its presence and advertise its sexual condition. Excited or reproductively-active monsters can transmit a detectable body odor which some people find offensive.

Another commonly held folk belief is that, when attacked, the Gila monster throws itself upon its back, or somersaults so that the head was where the tail had been. Some rural Mexicans also assert that the *escorpión* stings with its tail, and should always be approached head-on. Even educated people think that Gila monsters roll over like a shark to bite, thereby enlisting the aid of gravity to envenomate their opponents. This latter misconception is based on the fact that the venom glands are located in the lower jaws. The fact is, Gila monsters do not need to turn over on their back to deliver their poison as many a handler has found out to his or her dismay. Preparatory to biting, both the upper and lower teeth are bathed in venom-containing saliva secreted from glands in the lower gums.

An Indian practice, still prevalent in Mexico, is based on the seemingly indestructable nature of the Gila monster. To assure the lizard's death and prevent retaliation, either physical or supernatural, Yaqui Indians are said to kill the Gila monster by braining it with a huge stone or severing its head with a machete. This is to avoid touching the animal lest some of the venom come in contact with the skin, causing boils to erupt, the flesh to deteriorate, and eventual death. Then, the monster is hung by the neck or tail by a wire or string to a tree for several days, making sure that its feet are not touching the ground. Failure to follow this prescription can result in the monster's resurrection, and the animal taking vengance against its killers.

The tenacity of the Gila monster's bite has also generated its share of folklore. These include the belief that once the lizard has its victim in its grasp, it will not let go until sundown or until it thunders. It is also commonly assumed that an attached Gila monster cannot be released from its victim with human hands but must be pried off with the aid of a screwdriver, knife, or other tool. This latter statement, while somewhat of an exaggeration, is to be accepted as true if those who have one-handedly tried to disengage a determined monster from a throbbing finger are to be believed.

Other popular superstitions give the Gila monster extraordinary powers of gymnastics, the lizard "leaping fully two feet from the ground." Its forked tongue and flat, triangular-shaped head have also led some country folk to opine that the Gila monster is a hybrid cross between a lizard and a venomous snake. Additional myths attributed to the Gila monster include tales in which the forked tongue acts as a stinger, stories of the reptile biting out large chunks of flesh or clothing, and the legend that every letter of the alphabet can be found somewhere in the markings on its hide.

One of the most quizzical characteristics ever attributed to the Gila Monster was reported in the *Phoenix Herald* on June 18, 1880, and again on September 4th of that year. These accounts describe the Gila monster as asymmetrical, that is, having unequal halves like a flounder or a halibut. The basis for such statements is a mystery. Either the paper was reporting on an aberrant specimen, or the writers were exaggerating the tendency for the markings on some Gila monsters to appear disjointed along the indentation that marks the animal's backbone (Fig. 22).

Folklore That Might Be True: Some beliefs regarding Gila monsters, while sounding implausible, might yet be proven factual. Several people have told us of seeing unusually large numbers of Gila monsters in a particular year, and are of the opinion that these lizards are more active during some years than others. Other people are convinced that Gila monsters are most likely to be encountered immediately after drenching summer rains. We do not know if these statements have any basis in fact. It may well be that in years of poor food supplies, Gila monsters have to spend more time foraging than is usual, or that flooding causes enough animals to leave their burrows to be noticeable. Not enough studies have been done to determine if there are such things as "Gila monster years."

A common claim, made both in print and in casual conversation, is that captive Gila monsters become much more animated when taken out of their cages and placed in natural surroundings. This is certainly so of animals placed in sunlight, and biologists attribute this reaction simply to the animal's normal "heating-up" behavior. Some pet owners, nonetheless, maintain that this response occurs even when the animals are placed outside in the shade, and believe that this reaction is due to some innate intelligence reminding the animal of its "lost freedom." Again, we will let someone else decide the merits of their case.

An even more interesting tale was told to us by Mr. John Laird, curator for the Gila Bend Museum and a former employee of the Southern Pacific Railroad. He said that when he and other railroad workers would layover at a line station in Arizona's 40-Mile Desert northeast of Gila Bend, they used to throw the scraps of their breakfasts of bacon and eggs out into the surrounding desert. Over a period of several years they baited in and captured 22 Gila monsters, all of which were eventually set free when the station was abandoned. Regarding this story as just another "desert windy," we were surprised to read a letter to the editor by Ernest Griffith in the January 1955 issue of *Desert Magazine* stating: "In our camp in the Picachos there was a Gila monster who took up residence in a monument [rock cairn] and always showed up when he smelled bacon, for a strip of the rind." Such statements of Gila monsters being attracted to human food sources are bolstered by the lizard's reputation in Mexico as a chicken egg thief. *Quien sabe?*

Figure 22. Dorsal view of a Gila monster showing an asymmetry in markings between the left and right side, ca 1880. As shown by the triangular-shaped tail, this emaciated individual was near starvation prior to being mounted by a taxidermist. Photo courtesy of The Arizona Historical Society, Tucson

IS THE GILA MONSTER POISONOUS?

The Gila monster is an overgrown, variegated, perfectly harmless lizard.

Richard J. Hinton, *The Handbook to Arizona*, 1878

There is no question but that the venom of the Gila monster is more rapid and fatal than that of the rattlesnake.

Arizona Citizen (Tucson), July 25, 1885

Three decades after Edward Cope identified the Gila monster as a distinct species in 1869, a debate still raged over whether the animal was truly poisonous. Today, the venomous nature of the reptile is so well publicized that such a controversy might at first seem a little strange. After all, the Indian and Hispanic residents of the Southwest were well aware that the lizard was poisonous and Cope had suspected that it was -- so why were other Anglo-Americans so hard to convince? The scientists of the day, however, had every right to be cautious. Nowhere else in the world had anyone ever found venomous lizards. Moreover, the Gila monster and its Aztec relative have no hollow, hypodermic-like fangs for delivering venom, and, also unlike poisonous snakes, these lizards have no venom sacs in their upper jaws.

Not wanting to place their trust in folk-beliefs and stories told in frontier saloons and mining camps, researchers conducted experiments with captive Gila monsters. Laboratory techniques were then rather primitive, however, and the results were often inconclusive. To further complicate the scientist's inquiries, Dr. Robert Schufeldt was bitten by a Gila monster while conducting one of these experiments at the Smithsonian Institution in 1882. Although Dr. Schufeldt suffered some reaction to the bite, he concluded that the bite was essentially harmless, except for the damage done by the reptile's teeth. Needless to say, his conclusions were reported far and wide.

The following year, researchers Silas Mitchell and Edward Reichert reported that they had injected Gila monster saliva into frogs, pigeons, and rabbits, and that in every case the animals died within a few minutes. In 1885, a Tucson physician, Dr. John Handy, induced a captive Gila monster to bite a chicken -- the luckless bird died in about a minute. These experiments might have settled the matter in favor of the poison advocates, had not Dr. Henry Yarrow of the Smithsonian Institution published the results of his work with Gila monsters in 1888.

Dr. Yarrow found that rabbits and chickens injected with the lizard's saliva suffered little or no ill effects. Even more important, Yarrow reported that one of his laboratory assistants had been bitten several times by a Gila monster and had experienced no serious harm. Further support for the non-poisonous camp came in 1892. A Tucson doctor named George Goodfellow was bitten by a captured Gila monster, and after showing no symptoms of being poisoned, he became a strong advocate of the opinion that the Gila monster was harmless.

So what was going on? Why were the results of these experiments so contradictory? Most of the confusion resulted from the many variables involved with Gila monster venom collection techniques and the lack of controls available. The researchers were often working with Gila monster saliva, not venom *per se*, and they had no way of knowing if their samples were rich in venom or contained little poison. Because the Gila monster has no fangs, the amount of venom delivered to a subject is also uncertain and highly variable, and nearly venomless bites like those recieved by Drs. Schufeldt and Goodfellow are not uncommon. It was also not then known that the crucial factor in Gila monster envenomation is the length of time that the animal is able to "hang on" and chew venom into the wound.

After 1900 numerous laboratory studies were performed that conclusively showed that the Gila monster indeed has a poisonous venom. The American Southwest could now claim the distinction of being the home of a uniquely poisonous lizard.

POTENCY OF VENOM

No, the breath of the Gila monster will not kill steers grazing in the neighborhood. Its bite is poisonous...but the bite of the monster is not necessarily fatal. On this point I have made diligent inquiry of every "Hassayamper" I have met. By the way, an Arizona "Hassayamper" is a citizen who has lived here so long that he knows everything... The noun is Indian, and is the name of an "arroyo" or dry river bed near Phoenix. The Indians say whoever drinks of the water of the Hassayampa can never afterward tell the truth. The river has been an "arroyo" for a number of years, its waters having been consumed by eastern tourists and newspaper writers...

Arizona Graphic, September 23, 1899

Early researchers showed that Gila monster venom could kill small rodents, rabbits, fowl, and frogs, but definitive answers as to the potency of the venom proved as elusive as proving the saliva poisonous.

And for many of the same reasons -- difficulties in extracting uniform samples of venom, variations in individual Gila monsters, and different reactions in test animals all tended to confound experiments. Thus, the potency of Gila monster venom remained a source of speculation.

In 1913, the Carnegie Institution published the results of a number of experiments conducted on Gila monster poison. These studies documented the amounts of venom needed to kill mice and other warm-blooded mammals up to the size of a dog, and showed lethal dosages to range from .04 to .25 ccs of venom per kilogram of body weight, depending on the species of animal involved. As in the earlier studies, the results varied widely, not only between species, but between individuals.

In a later study of the effects of Gila monster venom on anesthetized guinea pigs and rats conducted at Arizona State College in the late 1940's, it was found that the action of Gila monster poison on these animal's respiratory and cardiac systems was relatively slow in comparison to other venoms. The average time for death from respiratory failure was just a little under two hours. Again, great individual variations were noted, and the results were difficult to evaluate.

Writing in 1983, researcher Findlay Russell found minimum lethal dosages of dried Gila monster venom injected intravenously into mice to range from about 0.50 to 1.0 milligram of poison per kilogram of body weight. Thus, *if* humans are as susceptible to the venom as mice, it would take a dose of from 32 to 70 milligrams of Gila monster venom to kill a 150-pound man. Since only about 17 milligrams of venom can be extracted from a large captive Gila monster, it therefore appears that the danger of an adult human dying from a Gila monster bite is slight.

Were Gila monsters able to produce as much venom as a large rattlesnake, the chances of a fatal encounter would be greatly enhanced. Although Dr. Russell found western diamondback rattlesnake venom to only be about half as potent as Gila monster poison, a large specimen of this snake may contain up to 600 milligrams of venom. It thus appears that Gila monster venom is neither especially deadly (when compared to such tropical snakes as cobras and kraits), nor is delivered in sufficient quantity to be life-threatening to a human.

On the basis of these experiments and a great many personal observations, Dr. Donald Kunkel, Medical Director of the Samaritan Regional Poison Center in Phoenix, considers the Gila monster's bite to be only mildly poisonous. Kunkel believes the Gila monster's venom is not as toxic as rattlesnake venom, or scorpion or black widow venom. It is well documented that a "normal" Gila monster bite does not kill an animal the size of a cat or larger. Yet many people are of the opinion that humans can, and have, died from the bite of a Gila monster. Is this so, and if so, under what circumstances?

65

REPORTS OF HUMAN DEATHS

"In the early '80's," stated Mr. George I. Burnside, "a Mexican and myself were traveling along the Gila River. It was the middle of June, and when the sun was well up we sought the inviting shade cast by the spreading leafy branches of a big willow tree near the bank of the river. We both stretched ourselves out and were soon fast asleep. I was suddenly awakened by a series of yells from my companion. To my astonishment I saw him jumping about wildly, and when he faced me my blood ran cold. There, hanging to the poor fellow's wrist, was a Gila monster fully twenty inches in length. He caught the squirming body of the reptile in his free hand and tried to pull it off, but it clung to his wrist with the tenacity of an English bull-dog. I hurried to his assistance and with my hunting knife made short work of the reptile. We had nothing to use as an antidote and were miles from anyone. It was useless to move. The Mexican displayed remarkable nerve, saying only once, 'it will all be over in an hour.' Night was just setting in as I commenced to push my way on toward Yuma after having witnessed a death that sometimes now I see in my dreams."

Arizona Sentinel (Yuma), July 28, 1894

Burnside's tale is typical of a number of similar frontier yarns that appeared in print around the turn of the century. In almost all of these accounts the victim is not named and the writer plays on a natural fear of being bitten by a venomous animal in a wilderness setting far from help. While fun to read, none of these stories is authenticated and all lack credibility. Nonetheless, there are a few reports in which the victim is named and which have been sufficiently documented so that some conclusions can be drawn as to whether a Gila monster's bite has ever been fatal.

Colonel Yeager: The following article first appeared in the May 2, 1884, issue of the *Cochise Record* newspaper, published in Tombstone, Arizona Territory, and was widely reported:

Sunday evening Dr. Mathews was summoned by telegram to Fairbanks [a now defunct settlement about ten miles west of Tombstone on the San Pedro River] to attend Colonel Yearger [Yeager], who was reported seriously ill. Owing to a

66

delay in the telegram the doctor did not reach the patient until several hours after his death which had been very sudden. It appears that Yearger had been fooling with a Gila monster, and in attempting to open the creature's mouth, was bitten on the right thumb. Instantly the poison took effect, and although every convenient remedy was applied, he lived but a few hours. An inquest was subsequently held, and a verdict returned in accordance with the above facts. As this is the third or fourth death which has occurred in the Territory from bites of this reptile, it should set at rest, at once and for ever, the theory so prevalent that their bite is not poisonous.

In the ensuing years, the story of Colonel Yeager was retold again and again, the scenario growing and becoming more lurid with each telling. It was soon a cornerstone of the argument in favor of Gila monsters being deadly. However, writing in the *Scientific American* in 1907, Dr. George Goodfellow threw cold water on what had previously been considered an open-and-shut case. Responding to a version of the story that had appeared in the magazine the previous year, Goodfellow wrote:

> The man [Yeager] was bitten and died, and I was one of the physicians summoned to attend him. The autopsy demonstrated cirrhosis of the liver, ascites [abnormal amounts of fluid in the abdomen], fatty heart, etc., and his history evidenced the cause of his death to be acute alcoholic poisoning grafted upon chronic alcoholism.

Since the Colonel was a known imbiber and had been administered copious quantities of the "prescribed antidote for snake bite" after being bitten, Goodfellow's assessment makes sense. The 55-year-old Yeager was not the first, nor the last patient to find the cure as, or more deadly than, the affliction. The individuals and circumstances of the other "three or four deaths" referred to in the *Cochise Record* article are unknown.

The Kansas Warden: The *Arizona Blade Tribune,* a newspaper published at Florence, a small town about 40 miles southeast of Phoenix, published this account on February 6, 1915:

Dies From The Bite Of A Gila Monster

The bite of a deadly Gila monster captured in the vicinity of Tucson and sent to the University of Kansas some time ago has caused the death of L. L. Dyche, fish and game warden of the state of Kansas and a well-known scientist of the University of Kansas. The animal bit Dyche and in ten days he died from heart failure. Physicians declared that his death was due to the bite of the Arizona reptile.

Taken by itself, this news item would seem to be a solid record of a death caused by the bite of a Gila monster. However, two obituaries for Dyche published in scientific journals made no mention of a Gila monster bite. A lengthy summary of Dyche's career as a scientific collector, zoology professor, and state game warden was presented in the February 19, 1915, issue of the prestigious journal *Science*. Like the other obituary, published in the *Auk* in 1917, it indicated that the Professor had been in poor health for some time and died of natural causes. Where the Florence newspaper got its story is a mystery.

Death of a Showman: The late Dr. Tracy Storer, former chairman of the zoology department at the University of California at Davis, published the following account in 1931. Because the case was investigated by the California Industrial Accident Commission and the hospital's records were preserved, the facts of the case were particularly well documented:

L. M. was a man employed at an amusement place on Main Street in Los Angeles. Some time in the summer of 1915 the management had purchased a Gila monster (*Heloderma* sp.) which was kept as one of the features of the show. Employees had been warned to leave the animal alone, not because of any possible danger to themselves, but because by injury to the animal its value as an exhibit might thereby be reduced. This order had not been enforced, and L. M. had been in the habit of taking the animal to the front of the place and displaying it in order to attract patronage to the show.

Having stated earlier to the proprietor and to other employees that he had been bitten by other Gila monsters used elsewhere in a similar capacity in the past, he entertained no particular fear of the animal. On August 16, 1915, he was holding the reptile in his right hand and at intervals tapping it on the nose with his left hand to induce the animal to open its mouth. Continuing this procedure his attention was distracted by a question from some bystander and on striking down, the index finger of his left hand dropped into the Gila monster's mouth. The reptile immediately clamped down on the finger, and, as is the habit of the species, held on with bulldog-like tenacity. Efforts to pry its jaws apart did not avail and so two other employees each seized a jaw and forced them apart so that the finger could be extricated. The man was not alarmed by the event but one of his associates recommended that the wound be treated and an effort was made to obtain a hypodermic syringe. This failing, he was taken to the Los Angeles Receiving Hospital where he came under medical attention.

As soon as the patient reached the hospital, which was about 15 minutes after having been bitten, the attending physician immediately applied a tourniquet to the afflicted (left) arm, to stop the flow of blood toward the heart. There were two small cuts on the left index finger. These were about half an inch apart and each one-eighth inch in length. Potassium permanganate solution was injected rather freely into the bitten finger around the bites and elsewhere, the physician believing that it was better to run the risk of losing the finger than of injecting an amount too small to be effective. Fifteen minims of digalen (a digitalis preparation) was given as a heart stimulant and then 37 ounces of warm normal saline together with 15 minims of adrenalin were administered by intravenous injection in the right arm. Also, a deep hypodermic of 1/120 grain atropine was given. About this time the patient gave a big convulsion and fell back. Stimulants were applied but to no avail. The patient rallied only to gasp a few times and then die. Death came about 51 to 52 minutes after having been bitten.

This account, at first glance, might seem to indicate a *bona fide* case of a death caused by a Gila monster bite. But as Dr. Storer pointed out in his article, the victim was an alcoholic, a drug addict, and had a long history of heart trouble. It is highly possible that the patient died as a result of an adverse reaction to the medications and intravenous injections received at the hospital. Once again, this is a case of a patient in poor health who received treatment that may have proved worse than the affliction.

A Fatal Farewell: This fantastic letter from a 70-year-old lady was received in the 1970's by Steve Prchal, then assistant curator of small animals at the Arizona-Sonora Desert Museum near Tucson:

Dear Steve: Here is a picture of my brother-in-law back in 1930 with a Gila monster he captured on the Bud Yoas Ranch (which is now the Agua Caliente Ranch). It is back east of Amado, Arizona [about 40 miles south of Tucson]. He collected Gila monsters as a hobby, and in those days you could sell them... In the 1930s there was a snake show in Tucson and my brother-in-law would sell them [Gila monsters] to her [a lady at the snake show], and one of the Gila monsters he sold to her had little ones and he asked if he could buy one of the babies from her. She sold it to my brother-in-law and she picked it up and held it close to her face to tell it good-bye and it latched on to her cheek. My brother-in-law grabbed it to keep it from turning over and it was so small it turned over anyway. My sister grabbed a knife to try to dig the jaws open and couldn't. They got the woman in the car and started for the hospital and she was dead before they got there. As you *know*, when a Gila monster latches on to you and turns over and starts pumping that poison into you, then it's sure death. They say they don't chase you. I have had them chase me and I have seen them chase my brother-in-law. They say there have been few deaths due to a Gila monster's bite, but the thing of it is, you're dead in about 10 or 15 minutes and they don't know how many people *never* make it back to report their bite.

This letter, rather than evidence of the Gila monster's deadly potential, is testimony to the wonderful fertility of the human imagination and the persistence of folk beliefs regarding this amazing reptile.

The Pickled Pool Player: On April 29, 1930, the *Arizona Republic* (Phoenix) carried the following story:

Top Reap, 62 years old, proprietor of the Moore Pool Hall, died at 12:20 o'clock this noon in the Casa Grande hospital, two hours after he had been bitten by a Gila monster. The attending physician said last night that he would give 'poisoning from a Gila monster bite' as the cause of death in submitting the death certificate.

Mr. Reap was playing with the animal in the pool hall when he was bitten. The animal had been brought into the hall by one of the patrons and several were standing around looking it over and discussing it when Mr. Reap appeared. He began tapping it on the nose, witnesses said, and upon being cautioned replied:

"Oh, it wouldn't hurt you even if it did bite."

The reptile snapped at Mr. Reap, scratching one of his fingers, those present declared. But Mr. Reap, they said, continued to tap the animal on the nose. They said that suddenly it snapped again and this time sunk its teeth deeply into Mr. Reap's thumb. It required five minutes to get the reptile loose, the men finally succeeding with the aid of a pair of pliers.

In the meantime, Mr. Reap became unconscious. He was taken to the Casa Grande hospital where he was given immediate care. He regained consciousness but his condition was weak and all further efforts to save him proved futile. He again lapsed into unconsciousness and died at 12:20 o'clock.

Dr. Laurence Klauber, a venomous reptile expert living in California, was interested in this incident, and obtained the following statement from an informant three months after the death of Mr. Reap:

> I investigated this, and it is all too true. Completely paralyzed within about 2 minutes. The Dr. said he never saw anyone throw up such stuff or pass from bowels. Said he could hardly stay with him. The man was drinking, and may have been quite drunk, so witnesses said.

An Absent Assassin: In 1953 a farmworker's baby was found bleeding and near death after having been left unattended at the edge of a cottonfield 20 miles southwest of Phoenix. It was believed that the child had been bitten by a venomous reptile, but no such animal could be found. The baby was taken to a hospital but died. Subsequently, a debate ensued between two venomous animal experts as to whether a Gila monster or a rattlesnake was to blame.

The year after the tragedy, M.D. and herpetologist Dr. Frederick Shannon published a detailed report describing the incident and the results of a postmortem examination. The following is his account, minus some technical medical terminology:

Report On A Fatality Due To Rattlesnake Bite

> On the evening of October 15, 1953, a 22-month old child was found unconscious in a cotton patch near Goodyear, Arizona. Although a distance of only 20-odd miles was involved, two hours lapsed before the patient was presented for treatment at Good Samaritan Hospital in Phoenix. The attending doctors, Thomas Bate and Sam Johnson, were told that when the parents found the child he was bleeding profusely from the right eye and from a puncture wound on the left side of the bridge of the nose. Five closely-spaced punctures on the right side of the chin and a superficial quarter-inch laceration on the right side of the lower lip were

present, but neither of these latter wounds was bleeding. There were no further breaks in the skin.

At the time of entry into the hospital, the child was still bleeding freely from the right eye and from the puncture wound on the nose. Massive ecchymoses [blood-engorged tissues] were present interorbitally [between the eyes] as well as down the left side of the face and, to a lesser extent, down the right. The right eye was so swollen that the lids could not be opened for the purpose of ascertaining the source of bleeding. Respirations were rapid and shallow, and the pulse was greatly accelerated, although the exact rate is unknown.

All attempts to control bleeding from the right eye were futile, and the eye, as well as the puncture mark on the nose, bled until death six and one-half hours after entry. It was realized by the attending physicians that the outcome would be fatal, but shallow incisions were made into the swelling by Dr. Bate in the hope that some of the venom could be extracted. Intermittent suction was instigated on the incisions until death ensued.

There was some question among the attending physicians as to whether the child had been killed by a snake and an autopsy was ordered. I was invited to be present and thus gained my first knowledge of the case.

Herbert L. Stahnke of Arizona State College at Tempe was also present at the autopsy. For some reason not disclosed to me, he came to the conclusion that the bite was inflicted by a Gila monster. This opinion is entirely inconsistent with all available evidence, and inasmuch as it would distort all the currently recognized facts about the poison and habits of the Gila monster to have the erroneous opinion (which was widely circulated over television) that a Gila monster could possibly have inflicted the type of death described above, I shall elaborate on the over-whelming evidence that the damage was done by a rattlesnake.

First, it is well known that the Gila monster does not have a closed system of injecting venom as does the rattlesnake and that the poison is elaborated (activated) by salivary glands in the lower jaw. For a considerable quantity of the venom to reach the circulation of a victim, the Gila monster must therefore hold on and chew, while the saliva haphazardly contacts the wound. It is currently recognized that the lizard has strong jaws, and if it does get a good hold on a victim the surface tissues of the victim are considerably mutilated. Yet the attending physicians state that the only visible perforations on the child were the one bleeding puncture mark on the nose, the five small linear perforations on the chin, and the small lip laceration. Perhaps Professor Stahnke did not hear the physicians state that the other incisions were surgically produced. The puncture marks on the chin are identical with those of the left lower jaw of a snake...

Secondly, the pathological findings are inconsistent with those which would have resulted from *Heloderma* poisoning but consistent with those of *Crotalus* [rattlesnake] poisoning...

Writing in 1970, Dr. Stahnke, director of the Poisonous Animals Research Laboratory at Arizona State University, gave a different version of what had been a widely reported incident:

One fatality apparently due to a venomous [Gila monster] bite should be mentioned. Shannon (1954) reported this death as due to rattlesnake bite. The victim, a two-year-old child of cottonpickers, was left to entertain itself while the family picked cotton near Goodyear, Arizona. An older brother was sent to check on the child's welfare only to find it bleeding profusely from the face and in a semi-comatose condition. One of us (H.L.S.), present at the autopsy, made two convincing observations; a series of small punctures in an arc on the chin of the child and severe periorbital hemorrhage [bleeding around the eye]. At the site of the accident the thick silty soil showed more disturbance than that produced by a snake. It appears as though the infant picked up the "visitor" and pulled the lizard up to its face to show it some affection.

We are inclined to accept Dr. Shannon's assessment of the case and do not believe a Gila monster was involved. Besides the time of year and the episode's location favoring a rattlesnake hypothesis, Shannon was a medical doctor (Stahnke was a zoologist) and better equipped to make a medical diagnosis. Ironically, Dr. Shannon himself was killed by a Mohave rattlesnake in 1965 while collecting reptiles in southeast Arizona. Although Shannon was flown to Los Angeles for treatment, all efforts to save him failed and he died a few hours after being bitten.

So, has a Gila monster bite ever resulted in a human death? The strongest case for such a conclusion is the demise of the Casa Grande pool hall operater in 1930. It should, nonetheless, be remembered that the primary source of information in this case is a newspaper article and not a detailed clinical report. Also, as was the case with Mr. Yeager and the circus showman, the victim was middle-aged or older, not in good health, and the effects of the bite were complicated by the victim's long and recent use of alcohol.

Interestingly, stories of human deaths from Gila monsters cease after the early 1930's. The best explanation for this phenomenon is not that fewer people are being bitten now, or that medical advances have prevented fatalities from Gila monster bites, but that medical authorities began keeping better records. As medical records improved, writers stopped reporting imaginative tales of suffering and death. An analysis of case histories shows that no person in good physical condition and spared harmful or misapplied medical assistance has ever died from the bite of a Gila monster.

SOME FAMOUS GILA MONSTER BITES

> Dr. Ward, of Phoenix, an old practioner in the valley, says: "I have never been called to attend a case of Gila monster bite, and I don't want to be. I think a man who is fool enough to get bitten by a Gila monster ought to die. The creature is so sluggish and slow of movement that the victim of its bite is compelled to help largely in order to get bitten."

> *Arizona Graphic*, September 23, 1899

Gila monster bites have always been newsworthy and a constant source of material for Southwest storytellers. The following "bite-stories" are some of the best known, and while each is based on fact to the best of our knowledge, most of them have been repeated so often that all of the versions may not be recognizable as having the same source. The stories presented are the earliest or otherwise the most reliable version available.

The Walter Vail Incident: This letter was sent to the Arizona State Historian on March 24, 1928, in an attempt to "set the record straight." It was written by Edward L. Vail and describes a Gila monster encounter involving his brother, Walter, many years earlier:

> My dear Major Kelly: In reply to your favor of the 19th I would say my brother Walter L. Vail, was bitten by a Gila Monster at the Happy Valley Ranch, which is located in the Rincon Mountains, on or about the 8th of May, 1890. Walter was attending a spring roundup at that ranch, which is about 40 miles north of his home ranch which is the Empire. In the morning, as they were driving in the cattle, he saw a large Gila monster and killed it, as he supposed, and tied it on the

74

back of his saddle, as he wished to show it to his partner, Mr. C. V. Gates, who had never seen one.

When he arrived at the roundup camp he found his saddle was loose and put his hand up on the cantle of the saddle to get off of his horse; the Monster seized the middle finger of his right hand and hung on like a bull dog. Mr. Bob Robinson who was with him was trying to kill the Monster with his pocket knife. Walter said to him, "Make a wedge and pry his mouth open," which he did.

As soon as he got his finger loose he asked Mr. Robinson to cut some strings off of his saddle and tie one around his finger and another around his wrist. Walter then cut the end of his finger to make it bleed, and dipped it into strong carbolic acid which they used for killing screw-worms. Walter rode to Pantano and telegraphed me to bring Mrs. Vail and come to Pantano. Dr. J. C. Handy met us there and approved of what my brother had done for himself. Dr. Handy put a rubber band on Walter's wrist and removed the saddle strings.

The doctor, Mr. and Mrs. Vail, and myself went to Tucson from Pantano on a locomotive [about thirty miles]. The doctor told us that the poison would attack the glands of the throat. About five p.m. Walter was quite sick and his tongue was so swollen that he could hardly articulate. This occurred soon after the doctor had taken off the last band from his wrist. Dr. Handy said when he reached Pantano he gave Walter a French remedy that would cause him to perspire freely and help throw off the poison. My brother soon recovered, apparently, but his throat was affected for some time after. Yours very sincerely, Ed. L. Vail.

P.S. I have written more than I intended; but there have been so many ridiculous stories published about this incident that I am very glad to give you the facts of the case, which I know to be true.

Edward Vail was certainly right about his brother's ordeal being told often and incorrectly. Versions of the story appear wherever Gila monsters are discussed. Walter Vail's Gila monster adventure spawned a whole genre of "stunned Gila monster tied to a saddle revives to bite cowboy" tales. Sometimes the victim is Walter Vail, sometimes it is an unnamed cattleman, and in one version he is a Mexican *vaquero*. In some tellings Vail suffers a withered arm as a result of his experience; in still another, he dies.

A Careless Collector: F. H. Snow of the University of Kansas at Lawrence spent three summers collecting reptiles in southern Arizona just after the turn of the century. The following is a straightforward, firsthand account of an incident on one of these trips that was published in the Transactions of the Kansas Academy of Sciences in December, 1906:

During the past summer, on July 26, 1906, I had the misfortune to be bitten on the ball of the right thumb by a Gila monster, one of a pair which had been captured some two weeks previously and kept in a large box awaiting our departure from camp upon our homeward journey. In the same box were also placed two specimens of a very large frog. Late one afternoon it was observed that one of the frogs had been bitten by one of the Gila monsters. The next morning the bitten frog was dead and its body had shrunken to half its former dimensions. This was the first indication I had observed suggesting that the *Heloderma* might be venomous.

When we broke camp the two Gila monsters were placed in a galvanized-iron, water-bucket, over the the top of which a towel was tied to prevent the escape of the reptiles. I sat upon the seat with the driver with this bucket in front of me between my feet. The motion of the wagon apparently disturbed the serenity of the reptiles, they soon began to attempt an escape by pushing their heads against the towel. Being fearful that they would accomplish their purpose, whenever the prominence caused by the upward pressure indicated the location of the head of one of the monsters, I would force it down by a rap with the handle of the driver's whip, or with my spectacle case. At last, becoming a little careless, I used my hand instead of the artificial tools.

In one of these careless movements, I was struck in the ball of the right thumb by one of the indignant reptiles, receiving six incisions, four of which were of considerable depth, from which blood flowed in considerable quantities. Fortunately the jaws did not close upon the thumb so that there was no crushing effect produced. I sucked the blood from the wounds until one of my associates, Mr. L. A. Adams, who had some years ago suffered severely from a rattlesnake bite, provided me with a vial of permanganate of potash, which was kept in contact with the wounds for about an hour.

No evidence whatever of poisonous effect from this bite was to be detected, and I began to doubt the venomous character of the reptiles, since, notwithstanding the prompt application of the proper remedies, it seemed inevitable that at least some faint trace of the poison should have been left. But unless the Gila monster were in fact a venomous reptile, how could its universal bad reputation be accounted for? I think I may say that, without a single exception, the residents of Arizona and Sonora believe the bite of the *Heloderma* to be a very dangerous infliction, and several instances were circumstantially related to me of ranchmen and cowboys who had suffered untold agonies and had narrowly escaped death after one of its vicious attacks.

Snow was not the first nor the last collector to be nipped by a poorly incarcerated Gila monster. In 1953, the aforementioned Dr. Frederick Shannon was bitten through a cloth sack containing a reluctant captive. Like Snow's infliction, Shannon's bite was not serious, and it may be that the cloth absorbed much of the monster's saliva. Also, neither of these men were "held on to" by the lizard. The permanganate of potash (potassium permanganate) used by Snow was an old remedy for snakebite -- it proved ineffective and is no longer recommended.

The Hitchhiker's Pet: When the *Arizona Republic* in Phoenix ran this news story in March, 1934, the editors could not have realized that over the next fifty years a dozen versions of the story would be retold in the printed media. Here is the original version:

Gila Monster Carried For Hours Bites Youth

WILLIAMS - Through the long afternoon of yesterday (March 16), through last night and well into the forenoon today, 20-year-old Barney Buffington of Amarillo, Tex., trudged northward along Arizona highways - unaware that the new-found "pet" he carried in the bosom of his shirt as he left the sagebrush of the desert was a poisonous reptile.

Then, shortly before noon today, the Gila monster in his shirt bit him - and tonight he lies critically ill here.

Hitch-hiking northward from Phoenix, the young man came across the Gila monster near Wickenburg. Perhaps fascinated by its unusual beaded skin, unaware that its bite is poisonous, Buffington picked it up, wrapped his handkerchief around it and placed it in the bosom of his shirt.

Then Buffington hiked on, with the hand of death figuratively "around his shoulders," carrying the reptile in his shirt all that day, throughout the night and well into this morning before it became irritated and sank its jaws deep into his abdomen.

The flesh came with the jaws when young Buffington tore it loose. Ten minutes later, miles from help as he stood at a point midway between Ashfork and Williams on Highway 66, Buffington became violently ill. But luck favored him, and a motorist picked him up and rushed him to Williams. A physician worked over him for an hour before he was pronounced temporarily out of danger.

By all reports, young Buffington recovered from his ordeal, sadder but wiser for his experience.

A Soused Soldier: Frederick Shannon M.D., always interested in venomous reptiles and the treatment of their bites, published this account in 1953. The incident took place at an army base, Camp Desert Rock, Nevada, and involved an 18-inch captive Gila monster that Dr. Shannon had acquired in Arizona:

On the night of March 19, 1953, an officer removed the Gila monster while the author was away and carried it to the officers' bar, where he proceeded to put on a wild animal show. The officer's cupidity, increased by recent imbibation of two beers, six martinis, and five Scotch-and-sodas, caused him to indulge in a game of Russian roulette, which was to have consisted of poking his right index finger into and out of the Gila mosnter's widely opened jaws. The first attempt was unsuccessful, and the lizard bit him firmly on the finger at the junction of the nail. After suffering three or four more good bites, each more distal than the preceding, the officer was able to pry loose his lacerated and freely bleeding finger. It was estimated that the lizard had indulged in a successful chewing time of some six or seven seconds.

After freeing his finger and being startled into momentary sobriety, the officer vigorously milked his arm, hand, and finger in an attempt to express as much venom as possible from the bleeding terminus. A rather tight tourniquet was applied within minutes to the finger, and for a feeling of extra security, two or three more were applied extending up to forearm. The tourniquets were removed at intervals during the 45 minutes following the bite which occurred at 10:30 p.m. and were off at the time of the author's arrival at 11:00 p.m. One of the medical aid men gave the officer 0.3 cc of adrenalin intramuscularly at 10:50, fearing that he would go into shock.

On arrival the patient was found sitting up on an examining table drinking coffee and suffering considerable pain. The pain had not been noticed until a few minutes preceding but was probably only masked as large amounts of alcohol are amazingly effective in producing effective analgesia. The patient was apprehensive and by 11:05 p.m. his pain was so severe that a quarter grain of morphine tartrate was given intramuscularly. As the patient was a large, young, strong, and obviously healthy male (75 inches, 220 lbs., 29 years old), incision and further application of the tourniquet were not employed. Difficulty was experienced in obtaining a good subjective history as the patient's sensorium was masked by alcohol. It was noted that his hand and the first three or four inches of his arm were moderately swollen, and that considerable swelling existed in the index finger. Both swelling and pain were greater than could have been caused by the tourniquet.

By 11:45 p.m. the effects of the adrenalin had diminished. The pain was pulsating in nature, shooting up the arm to the height of the deltoid insertion, while a steady burning pain was superimposed in the injured finger. At mid-night a half-grain of intramuscular codeine sulfate was administered. The pain increased steadily until 12:50 a.m. in spite of the morphine and codeine. As it was now felt that central nervous symptomatology due to the venom would be minimal, another quarter grain of morphine was given.

At 1:00 a.m. the lacerated finger was dressed and the patient removed by stretcher to his quarters. He was exhausted by walking a few feet to his bed. Within five minutes...the patient dropped off into an uneasy slumber. The patient slept throughout most of the next day, and when awake he was weak and dizzy and had a dull roaring in his ears. By the second day the patient was still slightly weak and tired easily, but he resumed his normal activities without undue fatigue. At no time since the second day has the finger hurt when at rest. The finger was slow in healing and on the day following the bite was still considerably swollen...by the third day the hand was improved to the extent that the patient tried using a screwdriver. At this writing, a week after the bite was inflicted, there is a local hyperesthesia [sensitivity of the skin] and pain to pressure.

The symptoms suffered by the officer, so carefully detailed by Dr. Shannon, are very typical of a case of envenomation by a Gila monster: the victim experiences excruciating pain, is dizzy and weak, and the area of the bite (almost always a finger) is swollen and very sore. The next day he feels much better but is still wobbly. In one or two weeks, he is back to normal and suffers no long term effects from the bite.

Innocent Victims?: Almost invariably, all documented cases of humans being bitten by Gila monsters involve men or boys picking up or handling the lizards. The vast majority of so-called victims are reptile collectors or researchers handling captive animals -- Robert Schufeldt, George Goodfellow, F. H. Snow, Frederick Shannon, Herbert Stahnke, and numerous other herpetologists were bitten by animals they were studying. Tales of hunters and travelers attacked by Gila monsters or waking up with one of the reptiles clamped on their wrists are not credible accounts. One wonders if anyone has ever been bitten by a Gila monster who was not handling or playing with the animal?

Two such cases of hapless victims have been widely circulated. One involves a motorcyclist (in some versions he drives a sports car), and in the other story the victim is a parachutist. Both incidents are based on statements made to Dr. Findlay Russell in the early 1960's. Now with the College of Pharmacy at the University of Arizona in Tucson, Dr. Russell was then a toxicologist with the Loma Linda University hospital in southern California where he treated the two men who had come to him for consultation as a leading venom authority. Both patients were either incredibly unlucky or both told the doctor fibs to cover their embarrassment for playing with what they knew to be a venomous animal.

According to Dr. Russell, the first young man that came to him was injured in this way: a couple of days earlier he had been riding his motorcycle along a raised embankment in a rural area near Yuma, Arizona. On one side of the embankment was an irrigation canal, on the other side was undeveloped desert. The man lost control of his motorcycle, tumbled off the raised roadway, and flew sprawling into the desert. On reaching his hand out to break his fall, he literally slid it into a Gila monster's mouth and was bitten!

Not long after the visit by the motorcyclist, another young man sought Dr. Russell's help for a Gila monster bite and his account was no less improbable. He was a sky-diver in an air show at a desert airstrip near Phoenix. On landing after a jump, a breeze caught the parachute and dragged him across a sandy mesa. He came to rest on top of a Gila monster which grasped him on the right shoulder! Both men recovered from their wounds without any serious consequences and with only bizarre stories to tell of their ordeals.

EFFECTS OF GILA MONSTER BITES ON HUMANS

"Son," the old cowpoke told me over the top of a double shot of redeye, "I'd rather sort bobcats than mess with one Gila monster."

Hal Moore, "Gila Monster -- Boris Karloff of the Desert," 1959

Gila monster bites are no longer so rare as to always make the newspapers.   According to Dr. Donald B. Kunkel, the Samaritan Regional Poison Center in Phoenix now treats an average of about one case a year. As indicated earlier, an objective analysis of documented cases of Gila monster poisoning suggests that the animals are dangerous but not deadly to an adult in good physical condition.   In addition to reviewing perhaps two dozen of these cases in the literature, we have personally interviewed several herpetologists who have been bitten.   While all of these people found the experience decidedly unpleasant, in no case did any of them consider themselves close to death. Many, like Dr. Schufeldt, experienced only minor symptoms, some were briefly hospitalized, and all soon recovered completely.

Gila monster venom is not a single chemical compound, but a complex mixture of proteins and other substances. Biochemists are still engaged in unravelling its mysteries.   In discussing its effects on humans, it might be useful to mention what it *does not* do: it does not produce paralysis of the arm or other affected part as was sometimes reported in early accounts; it does not affect the blood or inhibit its clotting ability as do some snake venoms; also, unlike rattlesnake venom, it does not contain digestive enzymes and will not destroy large amounts of tissue surrounding the bite. Only in two instances has Gila monster venom been known to produce an anaphylactic or allergic reaction in a patient.

What Gila monster venom *does* do is produce severe, excruciating pain at the point of the bite. The patient's blood pressure may drop with the result that he is in some danger of going into shock, although such a response, when it occurs, is usually mild in humans. A swelling of the affected part typically occurs. If a finger is bitten, as is often the case, the whole hand may become enlarged, the swelling often extending well up the arm. Often there is a bluish discoloration at the site of the bite. Severe bleeding commonly occurs, not because of any anti-coagulant properties of the venom, but because of the length and sharpness of the animal's teeth and the severity of its grip. The area around the wound is commonly very sensitive to the touch, and this tenderness may continue for some days after the wound has healed.

Patients usually experience weakness, dizziness, nausea, and excessive sweating. A few individuals have reported a ringing in the ears. The typical Gila monster bite victim suffers from pain for several hours, feels sick and weak for a couple of days, and recovers completely in a few weeks.

Unlike the bite of a rattlesnake, the bite of a Gila monster never results in amputation or the loss of the use of a limb. Nor is the Gila monster capable of injecting large amounts of toxin into a large vein as rattlesnakes have been known to do. Without fangs piercing a large vein, the Gila monster's poison cannot be quickly transported throughout the body causing death within minutes as was so often claimed in old newspaper accounts.

FIRST AID FOR GILA MONTER BITES

There are no proven first aid measures of value for helodermatid bites, other than disengaging the lizard as soon as possible.

Findlay E. Russell and Charles M. Bogert "Gila Monster: Its Biology, Venom, and Bite -- A Review," 1981

The following first-aid and medical procedures are those recommended by Dr. Donald B. Kunkel (Medical Director of the Samaritan Regional Poison Center in Phoenix), Dr. Findlay Russell (College of Pharmacy at the University of Arizona in Tucson), and Robert L. Smith (College of Agriculture at the University of Arizona). These experts are in essential agreement, and their recommendations are based on the best and most recent medical knowledge available.

While some Gila monster bites are mere nips, the removal of a lizard that has really clamped-down on a finger or other extremity is the first order of business. The monster will try to hold on firmly, and the longer it chews, the more venom will be released into the wound. There is no preferred method for accomplishing this chore. Some experts recommend prying the animal's jaws open with a screwdriver or other similar tool, some consider a pliers as the best equipment. Others suggest cutting the lizard's jaw muscles with a sharp knife. Pouring gasoline into the reptile's mouth has also been suggested, as has applying a flame to the underside of the creature. Most people, however, wind up removing the Gila monster by giving it a hard yank, therby causing additional tearing of the flesh and leaving some of the lizard's teeth embedded in the wound.

After the Gila monster is removed as quickly as possible, the wound should be rinsed in clean water, wrapped in cloth to staunch any bleeding, and the affected limb immobilized. The victim should then try to remain calm and promptly seek medical attention. No other first aid treatment should be attempted.

Some important "dont's" should be kept in mind. Additional cutting at the site of the bite in order to suck out some of the venom is not recommended. Nor is the use of a tourniquet. Aspirin may be taken, but the use of alcohol is to be avoided. The afflicted limb or member should *never* be packed in ice or immersed in ice-water. Owing to the likelihood of dizziness and weakness, the bite victim should avoid driving himself to the hospital or doctor unless absolutely necessary.

Once at the hospital, the usual procedure is to cleanse the wound and administer a tetanus shot. It is also a good practice to x-ray the bitten area for hidden tooth fragments. The patient is then given a pain-killer and hospitalized for observation. His blood pressure and pulse will be closely monitored and a intravenous saline solution may be administered to combat low blood pressure and possible shock. In some cases an antibiotic may be prescribed and a splint applied to the limb. Most patients will then be released after one or two days.

Rattlesnake antivenin, a substance that reacts chemically with rattlesnake venom and reduces its potency, is an important weapon in the doctor's arsenal for treating snakebite. Although two laboratories have produced experimental Gila monster antivenins, none of these products is commercially available. The infrequency of Gila monster bites and the lack of a demand have precluded development of such a product. As is the case with a scorpion sting, a child would be more susceptible than an adult to a Gila monster bite; however, with no record of a small child having been bitten, there really is no need for a Gila monster antivenin -- the lizard's bite is not normally life-threatening nor does it cause significant tissue damage.

ALCOHOL AS A REMEDY

The query is, was the *Heloderma* bite the cause of death or was it the whiskey so lavishly administered?

> Dr. Henry C. Yarrow, "The Bite of the Gila Monster," 1888

An old vaudeville gag went something like this: "A man bitten by a rattlesnake was made to drink whiskey until he could drink no more, on orders from his doctor. A couple of days later, he was seen wandering around in the woods. When asked what he was doing, he replied, 'I'm looking for another snake to bite me.'"

The use of whiskey to treat snakebite has been the source of jokes for so long that it is forgotten that doctors recommended it as the conventional treatment for venomous bites in the 1800's. Moreover, prodigious amounts of alcohol were often prescribed in the mistaken belief that persons suffering from snakebite could safely handle quantities of liquor that would harm a healthy man.

When Americans first came into contact with Gila monsters in the 1800's, whiskey was the antidote of choice. It was not until early in the 20th century that the medical profession began to realize that alcohol could be harmful to patients bitten by venomous animals, and came to reject the use of spirits as a treatment. Had doctors carefully reviewed the case of Colonel Yeager, and other drunks who had reportedly died from poisonous bites, they might have come to this conclusion much earlier. As it was, the folk belief that alcohol was a useful remedy for venomous bites persisted until well into the 20th century.

In the 1950's, Dr. Herbert L. Stahnke, director of the Poisonous Animals Research Laboratory, received a small grant from the National Academy of Sciences to study the effectiveness of alcohol as a treatment for venomous bites and stings. This is the same Dr. Stahnke who, you'll recall, apparently misdiagnosed the venomous bite inflicted on a farmworker's baby in 1953. Dr. Stahnke conducted experiments with scorpion venom, Scotch whiskey, and laboratory rats. The results of these tests must have appeared promising to him because in the mid-1960's he had one of his graduate students conduct more extensive experiments using not only scorpion venom, but rattlesnake and Gila monster venom as well. In this study, rats were injected with lethal and sub-lethal doses of the various venoms, and then measured amounts of alcoholic beverages were pumped into their stomachs through a tube. Beverages included diluted ethyl alcohol, Oso Negro vodka from Mexico, House of Stewart Scotch, Jose Cuervo tequila, and Johnny Walker cherry-flavored brandy!

If we have interpreted the results of the study correctly, the administration of spirits prolonged the time it took the animals given lethal doses of Gila monster venom to die, but did not prevent death. The effect of the cocktails on the animals given sub-lethal doses of venom is not clear, but it appears that, in the long run, administering alcohol neither helped nor hurt the rats in their battle with Gila monster venom. Although the student, who's thesis was accepted as part of the requirements for a master's degree, recommended additional study of the effects of alcohol, no other experiments in this vein are known to us.

DR. STAHNKE AND THE POISONOUS ANIMALS RESEARCH LABORATORY

In all treatment, including first aid, the cardinal rule is to do no harm.

C. H. Lowe, C. R. Schwalbe, and T. B. Johnson, *The Venemous Reptiles of Arizona*, 1986

Modern first-aid manuals sternly warn victims of poisonous reptile bites against subjecting a limb to extreme cold. To understand why these admonishments are given, we must review the ideas and career of Dr. Herbert L. Stahnke, Ph.D.

In the 1950's no biologist was better known in Arizona than Dr. Stahnke. Stahnke's fame was based on his reputation as a venomous animals authority and his perceived expertise in the treatment of poisonous bites and stings. Today, Dr. Stahnke's methods of treatment have been totally rejected by the medical community. Nonethelesss, the once widespread acceptance of his recommended treatment is an important part of any venomous animal story as well as an interesting study in human frailty.

Stahnke moved to Arizona from Chicago in 1928 and began teaching at a high school in Mesa, then a small farming community east of Phoenix. Here he became interested in scorpions, common poisonous animals in Arizona. At that time many people lived in rock or adobe houses out in the desert and children commonly went barefoot. Scorpion stings were a frequent occurrence, and occasionaly a small child might even die from a scorpion sting. As with all poisonous animal deaths, such incidents made headlines in the newspapers. What to do if bitten or stung was of great interest to Arizonans.

Herbert Stahnke was soon caught up in the scorpion hysteria, and he threw himself into the study of venomous animals. He began to experiment with antivenins to counteract the effects of the stings -- a topic that got him much publicity in the local press. Graduate studies during the summers of the 1930's resulted in his receiving a doctor's degree in biology from Iowa State College in 1939. The subject of his thesis was scorpions, and he became recognized as a leading authority on the poisonous beasts.

In 1941, Dr. Stahnke joined the faculty of Arizona State Teachers College at Tempe, later to become Arizona State University. An energetic man with a forceful personality, Stahnke was soon head of the rapidly expanding college's Division of Biological Sciences. College administrators and Arizona politicians saw a winner in Dr. Stahnke and his interest in scorpions, rattlesnakes, Gila monsters, and other poisonous creatures. In the late 1940's the Poisonous Animals Research

Laboratory was founded with Stahnke as director. Before long his laboratory was busily involved in the study of venomous animals and in the preparation of antivenins. His work was extremely popular with both the public and the press, and he was putting Arizona State College on the map, so to speak. Unfortunately, Dr Stahnke's charisma was no guarantee that his ideas were sound.

In 1953, Stahnke published a brief paper entitled "The L-C Treatment of Venomous Bites and Stings." L-C stood for "ligature and cryotherapy," a ligature being a tight tourniquet and cryotherapy meaning to treat with cold. This treatment was based on the long-known principle that chemical reactions are slower if temperatures are decreased. Stahnke reasoned that the toxic effects of venom would be slowed or halted if the affected part was isolated and subjected to extreme cold. His recommended treatment was to place a tight tourniquet between the site of a bite and the heart, and then immerse the affected body part in ice-water "for at least two hours." More specifically, "for the Gila monster, six to seven hours was found necessary," according to Dr. Stahnke. Unfortunately, the action of venom on human tissue is not a simple chemical reaction, and extreme cold can be more damaging than venom. Nonetheless, Stahnke's L-C treatment was ballyhooed by the popular press from coast to coast as the latest word on what to do if bitten by a venomous animal.

Almost immediately, some medical doctors and researchers saw the danger of Stahnke's technique. Dr. Frederick Shannon, who, as we have noted, would challenge Dr. Stahnke's expertise on more than one occasion, published a paper the same year condemning cryotherapy. He concluded his presentation with the dire prediction that, "If a patient...should be subjected to the Stahnke treatment, amputation would undoubtedly be necessary. It should be concluded that the 'L-C treatment'... should be rejected *in toto*." But his warnings fell largely on deaf ears. Stahnke was too well known and too popular for his thesis to be rejected. The Poisonous Animals Research Laboratory was receiving national attention and helping to convert Arizona State College from an obscure normal school into a respected research institution. With supporters in high places, Stahnke's methods were immune to criticism. Arizona State printed thousands of booklets detailing the L-C treatment which were distributed far and wide.

Dr. Shannon valiantly continued to oppose cryotherapy until his death in 1965. Nor was he alone. In 1959 and again in 1961, Dr. Henry Limbacher, a Tucson physician, and Dr. Charles H. Lowe, a herpetologist at the University of Arizona in Tucson, co-authored papers critical of cryotherapy. At about the same time, toxicologist and venom expert Dr. Findlay Russell began publishing articles questioning the value of Stahnke's teachings. But articles in scientific journals pointing out that Stahnke had never presented meaningful clinical data to support his claims could not counteract the popular media, even within the medical community. Stahnke's lectures were as popular as ever, and he appeared on numerous television shows including the national program "What's My Line?" In 1966, Arizona State University published Stahnke's "The Treatment of Venomous Bites and Stings," a 117-page handbook on cryotherapy. Thousands of copies of the book were distributed, and the "cold-treatment" of venomous bites was widely practiced.

Then, in the late 1960's, the tide began to turn against cryotherapy. Phoenix newspapers, which had much more influence with the general public than articles in scientific journals, began reporting that experts disagreed with Stahnke's L-C treatment and believed it to be harmful. Angry letters of rebuttal followed, but the challenge to cryotherapy could not be ignored. Some physicians were getting the message in a decidedly disagreeable way. Writing in 1971, researchers N. C. McCollough and J. F. Gennaro reported: "...no death or amputation in 112 cases of snakebite given antivenin, whereas eight of nine patients treated with cryotherapy suffered loss of the envenomated part...major amputations caused by snakebite continue to occur and physicians who have used cryotherapy are, at this writing, under suit for malpractice or being so threatened." Herbert Stahnke retired from Arizona State University in 1972, still defending his L-C treatment and the work of the Poisonous Animals Research Laboratory.

Today, Arizona State University is a large, modern institution, respected for its academic standards and research capability. The Poisonous Animals Research Laboratory has been largely disbanded and its only product is small quantities of scorpion antivenin for local distribution. Dr. Stahnke died in 1990 at the age of 87. His obituary in the *Arizona Republic* referred to him as a zoologist and a teacher and made no mention of cryotherapy or the controversy it generated within the medical community. All of the books on venomous bites and stings published in recent years warn readers not to immerse body parts for long periods of time in ice-water.

DANGER TO PETS AND LIVESTOCK

The *Virginia City Enterprise* of a recent date contains an account of a Gila monster captured by a man by the name of Blackheath which stood two feet high and seven feet long. The reptile is reported to have killed one of his dogs and got hold of the fore leg of another and broke it before his hold could be released...

Arizona Sentinel (Yuma), September 15, 1883

Although 19th century claims of Gila monster's attacking mules and other forms of livestock can be placed under the heading of folklore, there are a few valid accounts of dogs being bitten by Gila monsters. Most of these are anecdotal in nature, so biologist David Gorsuch's detailed account of a 16-inch Gila monster biting a small dog on April 16, 1932, south of Tucson is of some interest. According to Gorsuch, the dog's right foreleg was fractured and the reptile's teeth marks were clearly visible at the point of the break. This indicated either that the monster actually broke the leg two inches above the paw, or that the dog had fractured his leg in an attempt to shake off its tormenter. After a splint was applied to the break, the dog exhibited no serious signs of discomfort. Except for some discoloration at the site of the wound and a slight limp which soon disappeared, the dog was well on the way to recovery when Gorsuch again saw the animal 10 days later. No effects of poisoning were noted.

Because few bird dogs are afield during April and May when Gila monsters are most active, encounters between hunting dogs and Gila monsters are unusual. Tom Boggess, a Phoenix veterinarian and avid bird and mountain lion hunter, had one of his pointing dogs come running back to him with a Gila monster attached to its jowl while quail hunting on the Gila River Indian Resrvation south of Phoenix. He pried the lizard loose and released it unharmed under a mesquite tree. The dog resumed hunting with no apparent ill-effects from being bitten. Although many bird hunters and houndmen take their dogs to Tom for treatment, he has yet to have an animal brought to him because of a Gila monster bite.

Dr. W. L. Minckley, a biologist at Arizona State University, has conducted numerous field studies during the warm months of the year when Gila monsters are out. He told us that his black Labrador retrieved Gila monsters on two occasions without showing any signs of being bitten. Nor did his dog hurt the monsters.

It appears that actual attacks by dogs on Gila monsters are rare. One early Tucson resident reported that he could not goad either his cat or a rat-catching dog into taking on a tethered Gila monster. A case in which both a high school student and his dog were bitten by a Gila monster on the Tucson-Sells highway in 1953 is therefore of interest. The boy's dog got to the Gila monster first, and in the process of worrying it, was bitten on the face. The boy then put the lizard into a sack where it bit him on the thumb through the cloth. While the boy's thumb swelled and became very sore for a couple of days, the dog exhibited no adverse reaction to the bite other than vomiting that night. No one that we know has ever reported a dog killed or even seriously injured by a Gila monster, and pet owners have little to fear from this reptile.

HOMEOPATHIC USES OF GILA MONSTER VENOM

It would seem that in *Heloderma* we have a valuable remedy
for certain forms of paralysis... The patient took but a few
spoonsful, as she said it made her feel badly and she stopped
taking it. She complained of a sensation of the most intense
coldness in the paralyzed side. She died within a couple of
days.

Thomas L. Bradford, *Homeopathic Recorder*, 1895

Certainly one of the most bizarre aspects of Gila monster lore was
the belief that the animal's venom could be a remedy for paralysis and
other ailments. Such uses of animal poisons and other extraordinary
substances as cures come under the heading of the psuedo-science of
homeopathy, which has its origins in the late 18th century teachings of
S. C. F. Hahnemann in Germany. The underlying principle of
homeopathy is "like cures like." Practitioners treat ailments by
administering small doses of potent drugs that cause symptoms in
healthy persons similar to those produced by the affliction. Belief in
this semi-mystical practice survives to this day.

In 1890, a homeopathic practitioner living in Phoenix wrote in the
Homeopathic Recorder that the bite of a Gila monster produced
symptoms similar to those of paralysis agitans (Parkinson's disease) and
locomotor ataxia (paralysis and tremor due to advanced syphilis).
Homeopathists, long intrigued by the sinister power of venoms, eagerly
sought samples of Gila monster saliva to use on paralyzed patients.
Thus began a lively trade in Gila monsters and their venom throughout
the world.

In 1893 a 60-year-old homeopathic investigator with the unlikely
name of Robert Boocock experimented upon himself by swallowing a
few drops of highly diluted Gila monster venom. As he reported in the
Homeopathic Recorder, the results were disturbing, yet promising:

I was seized with such an internal coldness from my heart as
if I was being frozen to death internally... Last night whilst
retiring had some sharp shooting pains in my bowels, more on
the left side of the abdomen, and a sharp twinging in left
testicle. During the night had some erection of penis, but felt
too tired to take advantage.

A few days later Boocock noted additional symptoms which he
attributed to the new drug he eventually hoped to market:

89

Am very weak, very nervous. No headache, but a sore feeling. A desire to be quiet. Copulation long and very enjoyable. A large flow of semen... Oh, how powerful is this new poison!

Despite Boocock's thinly-veiled promotion of Gila monster venom as an aphrodisiac, most homeopathists continued to concentrate on using the poison in what to them was a more conventional manner. To the distress of postal authorities, literally hundreds of Gila monsters were sent to the East and to Europe prior to World War I in the search for a cure for paralytic illnesses:

One of Mr. Balke's [a Phoenix reptile dealer] best customers is the Imperial Prussian Clinic, which for the last three years has been conducting experiments with Gila monster venom. The German physicians believe that in this poison they have discovered a cure for locomotor ataxia. Mr. Balke has shipped the clinic over a hundred and fifty monsters in lots of a dozen.

Ernest Douglas, "The Gila Monster, a Convicted Suspect," *Arizona* magazine, December, 1910.

In spite of a statement made by an Arizona Game and Fish Department spokesman in 1952 that "studies now being conducted in Dr. Stahnke's laboratory are of definite therapeutic value and may some day aid medical authorities in combatting cancer and other human diseases," no reliable investigator has ever discovered a valid therapeutic use for Gila monster venom. Nor, unfortunately, has anyone ever confirmed Robert Boocock's claims for having discovered a Gila monster love potion.

COMMERCE IN GILA MONSTERS

It was no uncommon sight in former years to see Mexican and Indian boys trailing the hideous things at the ends of strings along the streets of towns and settlements in Arizona, taking care always to keep their bare feet out of the way of the uncanny-looking lizard. Sometimes, too, Gila monsters, strapped to a board like planked shad, would be offered for sale at prices ranging from a medio (6 1/2 cents) to a toston (50 cents), with few or no buyers.

> Frank Oakley, "Ugly as Sin Itself," *San Francisco Chronicle*, June 15, 1893

A commerical trade in Gila monsters began almost as soon as Americans began arriving in the Southwest in the 1860's. Initially most of the customers were proprietors of store-front menageries or private collectors (John Spring claimed to have captured or purchased nearly 100 Gila monsters in Tucson during the late 1860's and 1870's). By the 1880's a brisk commercial trade had developed:

> Gila monsters are quoted in the Tucson Market at fifty cents to a dollar apiece, according to size.

> *Mohave Miner* (Kingman), September 9, 1887

As the fame and reputation of these noteworthy lizards spread, so did the market, and by the 1890's many Gila monsters were being sent to buyers on the Pacific Coast, the East, and to Europe. At least one entrepenuer, E. L. Wetmore, was a dealer in Gila monsters, and his periodic shipments to New York regularly made the Tucson newspapers. According to the following column, however, the supply soon exceeded the demand:

> More Gila Monsters have been brought to town this year than during the entire previous three years. Mr. E. L. Wetmore who does most of the purchasing reports them a drug on the market, Eastern buyers generally having been supplied.

> *Arizona Citizen* (Tucson), July 17, 1894

By the late 1890's, either the supply had diminished, or business was picking up:

> Gila monsters are reported scarce in the market this year. One dealer has about forty Eastern orders, but cannot fill them through lack of reptiles.

> *Arizona Citizen*, November 1, 1897

An article in the September 23, 1899, issue of the *Arizona Graphic* states that "They [Gila monsters] range in price from four bits, Mexican, to $4.00, American, according to size, condition, and the necessities of the Indian merchants."

At this time most of the market was in the sale of live Gila monsters to institutions for use in medical and homeopathic experiments, or to side-shows and menageries for exhibition purposes. And while some shipments, such as those to the Imperial Prussian Clinic, might involve dozens of reptiles, the drain on regional populations was probably modest. Dead animals had little or no value, as the hides, while attractive, were small and made poor leather; besides, the animal was relatively scarce and difficult to skin. This was all to change with the coming of the automobile and the proliferation of roadside zoos and reptile gardens (Fig. 23.).

Figure 23. Roadside gas station, store, and reptile menagerie on U. S. Highway 70 near Safford, Arizona, ca. 1930. Photo courtesy of the Arizona Historical Society, Tucson.

In 1924, a prescient article in the *Arizona Republican* (Phoenix) optimisticaly predicted the benefits of a coming boom with the headline: "Enterprising Phoenician sees big future in Gila monster business so is establishing reptile gardens." The account then described how one could get started in such an enterprise, as a local dealer had a "selection of 200 of them for you, all alive and happy and fat and any size you wish...He is equipped to do business with the person seeking a collection as well as he who just wants a monster, say for a pet." If you were more interested in the supply-side of the coming industry than the exhibition side, the article concluded with the inducement that "Homesteaders, prospectors, roadbuilders and health seekers have sold several thousand dollars' worth of the reptiles and the demand is increasing steadily."

Not only were captive Gila monsters soon much in demand for display in "dens of death," the increasing numbers of Southwest tourists made the sale of Gila monster mementos a growth industry. While some Gila monster skins were made into hatbands, billfolds, belts, and even a handbag or two, the most common souvenir was a mounted, or rather stuffed, Gila monster leering from a cholla-skeleton perch or lamp base (Fig. 24).

Figure 24. Mounted Gila monster curio from the 1940's at the Buckhorn Museum, Mesa, Arizona.

By 1930, live animals were being offered in Phoenix at from $2.50 to $7.00 according to size, and mounted specimens were available at prices ranging from $5.00 to $7.50. Moreover, the advent of the Great Depression would soon make any source of income that could be gleaned from the desert worthwhile. More than a few foot-loose desert rats tried to eke out a living during the 1930's and 1940's hunting not only Gila monsters, but any reptile with a price on its head. One of these was Mr. Paul W. Hiegel. Then living in Tucson, Heigel and his partner would roam the surrounding countryside looking for Gila monsters and rattlesnakes which they captured with a wire lasso attached to a saguaro rib. Operating out of a central camp, they would keep their catches in a pit about six feet deep with rocked up sides. Since their animals were sold alive, they soon learned to keep the Gila monsters and rattlers separated as the Gila monsters would kill the snakes. Most of his Gila monster customers were tourists from back East, some of whom would take their purchase to a Tucson taxidermist for mounting as a mantlepiece. The average price received for Gila monsters had by then dropped to only about $1.50 apiece unless the catch was an exceptionally big one, and Hiegel made most of his money selling rattlers at 25 cents a pound to a dealer in Florida who marketed their venom.

CHANGING ATTITUDES TOWARD GILA MONSTERS

...although it [Gila monster] appears to have no real economic value, there are many who advocate its preservation. True, it is strictly a poisonous reptile, but its habits prevent it from being a real menace to man...these few unsavory traits can hardly give us cause to condemn to death such an interesting desert curiosity.

O. N. Arrington, "Notes on the Two Poisonous Lizards with Special Reference to *Heloderma suspectum*," 1930

Although the Gila monster has always attracted the attention of scientists and journalists, many Southwest settlers regarded this curious creature with loathing and contempt. To them, it was just another desert creepy-crawler in the same league with centipedes, tarantulas, Hualapai tigers (kissing bugs), and all-too-many rattlesnakes. If not seized for a captive, the animal was almost always killed when encountered, if not for posing an immediate danger, then out of fear that it might injure some child or pet in the future. This attitude, while less prevalent today, has not entirely gone away.

Herpetologist Charles Painter of the New Mexico Department of Game and Fish, reported to us recently that while traveling rural highways in southwest New Mexico he had encountered Gila monsters that were killed along the road without being run over. "It seemed clear," Painter said, "that someone had pulled over, walked back, and beat hell out of these lizards with a stick." Traditionally, few Gila monsters have been left in peace, and as early as the 1870's some people were predicting the lizard's eventual extinction along with wolves, grizzlies, mountain lions, and Apaches.

Before game management graduated to a science in the years following World War II, the Gila monster was accused of more than crimes against humanity. From 1900 through the 1940's predator control was considered essential if game populations were to recover. Besides such predators as wolves and coyotes that preyed on big game animals, hawks, owls, pack-rats, bobcats, ground squirrels, and even non-venomous snakes were persecuted as killers of game birds or destroyers of their nests. Given its reputation as a consumer of quail eggs, the Gila monster was roundly condemned, along with the roadrunner, as a hindrance to quail abundance.

Determining the effects of predators on quail numbers was therefore an important objective of the first scientific study of Gambel's quail. In a "diligent search" for Gila monsters over two nesting seasons in the early 1930's, David Gorsuch was able to find an amazing 37 of these reptiles in his study area on the Santa Rita Experimental Range south of Tucson. None of the lizards contained quail eggs. He concluded that the relatively few eggs that might be taken by these lizards would not limit quail numbers. No longer could the Gila monster be viewed as an enemy of the quail hunter.

The Gila monster was also receiving assistance from several champions who considered the creature an interesting and generally harmless member of the Southwest's fauna. In 1930, O. N. Arrington published a paper on the natural history of the Gila monster in which he advocated not only tolerating the animal, but preserving it -- the first call for protecting Gila monsters that we have found. Charles Vorhies, a University of Arizona wildlife professor, was more emphatic. In a write-up of Arizona's reptiles in a 1936 University of Arizona Bulletin, he rebuffed the "downright lies" then circulating about the animal, and concluded with the admonishment, "Should this species be exterminated we would be the loser." In the coming years, articles and statements such as these, repeated again and again, would gradually counteract the monster's undeservedly evil reputation.

No one, however, did more to champion the cause of the Gila monster than the aforementioned Dr. Herbert Stahnke of Arizona State College, who carried on an enlightened battle in promoting protection for the lizard. In the 1940's and 1950's, Dr. Stahnke conducted hundreds of lectures and programs on Arizona's venomous animals, which were extremely popular with the public. So effective were these presentations in raising the public's level of consciousness about the Southwest's venomous animals, that the facts regarding the Gila monster's harmless nature if left alone became generally accepted. By the time Dr. Stahnke proposed legislation protecting the Gila monster in 1950, there was little opposition to what was then an unorthodox action.

LEGAL PROTECTION

Roadside zoos and reptile gardens remained conspicious features of Southwest highways through World War II, and it was feared that the traffic in reptiles was causing Gila monsters to become scarce. When Dr. Stahnke began taking herpetology students on field trips in the Salt River Valley around Phoenix, it was not uncommon for them to capture two or three Gila monsters on each trip. By 1947, however, his prime areas were no longer producing specimens. Stahnke attributed this decline in success to overharvesting by commercial collectors who were paying from 25 to 50 cents an inch for Gila monsters. These animals were then sold to out-of-state dealers for between one and two dollars an inch -- $40 for a very large monster. Stahnke petitioned the Arizona Game and Fish Commission to protect the animal, which he feared was in danger of extermination, along with horned toads, large numbers of which were then being sold as pets.

On April 3, 1950, the three-man commission entertained a proposal to protect the lizards as Dr. Stahnke requested. Although one of the commissioners expressed his concern that Gila monsters might be damaging bird's nests on his ranch south of Tucson, a motion to prohibit the taking, sale, or possession of Gila monsters and horned toads without written permission passed unanimously. A one year grace period was given to anyone already having one of the animals in captivity. Two years later, the commission reaffirmed its action, passing a permanent Commission Order prohibiting the taking and sale of Gila monsters and horned toads without specific permission. Arizona thus became the first state to protect a poisonous reptile.

Fear of commercial collectors' moving into Nevada prompted that state to pass a law protecting Gila monsters in 1969, Utah followed in 1971, and New Mexico in 1975. There the lizard was listed as a state endangered species "likely to be in jeopardy within the foreseeable future." By 1980, the Gila monster was also protected in California and had been listed by the U. S. Fish and Wildlife Service's Office of Endangered Species as a species "possibly threatened with extinction, but about which there is not enough information to determine its status" -- a classification since upgraded to "now considered to be more abundant and/or widespread than previously thought." Should new information suggest that the Gila monster is undergoing a decline in numbers or distribution, or is under a substantial threat, it will be classified as endangered or threatened.

To further protect the lizard from exploitation, the Gila monster is included in the Convention on International Trade in Endangered Species (CITES) as a species which may become threatened if trade is not regulated to avoid over-harvesting. Mexico has recently become a signatory to CITES, and the Gila monster is totally protected in that country and may not be molested, sold, or exported from its home states of Sonora and Sinaloa. Thus, it is now illegal to kill or capture a Gila monster without a permit throughout its range.

Nonetheless, a substantial demand exists for the lizard as an exotic pet, and there remains a significant illegal traffic in Gila monsters to this day. Why this is so is difficult to explain. The animal, while exhibiting some individuality and an undeniable charm, even to the point of allowing itself to be handled and petted if given gentle treatment, is never to be completely trusted. Many of the bites that have occurred have happened while handling normally docile pets who "knew their owner well." Moreover, the Gila monster makes a lethargic captive, spending most of its time sleeping or otherwise doing little of interest. They are also difficult to propagate in captivity -- only a few institutions such as the Arizona-Sonora Desert Museum, the Oklahoma City Zoo, and San Diego Zoo have succeeded in doing so. As Arizona Nongame Branch Supervisor Terry Johnson states, "Certain people just desire unusual and forbidden reptiles with the same intensity that drives others to collect original paintings, rare stamps, and one-of-a-kind Indian artifacts."

According to Johnson and other herpetologists, the reptiles most in demand as pets and receiving the highest prices are rare venomous snakes and Gila monsters. Arizona Game and Fish records show 284 citations issued for reptile violations between 1983 and 1990, with 150 cases resulting in convictions. Almost all of the violaters are white males under the age of 40. Approximately half of the average 20 convictions a year involve Gila monsters. U. S. customs officials confiscate about another five Gila monsters a year at the Nogales and Lukeville border stations on the Arizona border with Sonora, and wildlife officers estimate the number of illegal Gila monsters in circulation in the Southwest during any given year ranges between 30 and 40. Some think the number is much greater.

Selling contraband Gila monsters can be lucrative. Several professional collectors are known to make visits to Gila monster country each spring under the guise of being bird-watchers or hikers. Any Gila monsters obtained are then traded to other reptile pet owners or sold to dealers for prices ranging between $150 and $200. A dealer with connections can then sell the lizard to a Japanese or German collector for a considerable profit. For example, a recent catalog offered reticulate Gila monsters for $975, with banded specimens going for $1,375!

Because professional collectors usually only deal with customers they know, violators are difficult to apprehend. Undercover officers for wildlife agencies know that many collectors ship their catches to buyers in airline baggage labeled "harmless reptiles." To catch some of these law breakers, the Arizona Game and Fish Department operated a "sting" from 1986 to 1988 out of a dummy dealership called "The Black River Trading Company." During this time, undercover agents purchased around two dozen Gila monsters from collectors at $75 each, and through advertisements in reptile club newsletters, sold them to out-of-state dealers at prices ranging from $150 to $400 apiece. Both the collectors and the dealers were then arrested.

Gila monsters are also captured and taken out of the wild for other purposes. Between 25 and 50 of the lizards are turned into Arizona's wildlife rehabilitation center each year by construction workers, rural homeowners, disenchanted pet owners, and ignorant hikers. Few of these animals are suitable for release back into the wild, and most wind up as specimens in scientific institutions, bait for law enforcement "sting" operations, or as educational exhibits. Among the best places to see captive Gila monsters today are the Arizona-Sonora Desert Museum near Tucson, the Arizona exhibit at the Phoenix Zoo, and the living reptile display in the Biological Sciences building at Arizona State University. These, and other facilities, have properly-cared-for animals in attractive surroundings open to the public.

Like the animals they are designed to protect, state and federal reptile laws are not to be trifled with. Substantial fines of several thousand dollars have been levied against offenders and some collectors have received prison sentences. One violator caught napping with 14 Gila monsters and other contraband reptiles in Sonora, Mexico, was jailed in 1990 and faced a possible nine-year sentence and $60,000 in fines. Clearly, Gila monsters are best left alone.

THE GILA MONSTER IN LITERATURE AND FILM

The creature raised its head. Blood and bits of warm, wet flesh slipped from the mouth, down onto the bed and the naked girl. An overwhelming rotting odor flooded the room, and Maria began to pray as the orange-and-black creature

98

opened its mouth to let what remained of her lover's body slip
out...to make room for her...

Gila!, a novel by Les Simons, 1981

Until very recently the Gila monster fared poorly in the popular
media. Early newspaper articles usually portrayed the lizard as an
oddity if not an outright freak, and invariably focused on its poisonous
properties, both real and imagined. Myths and tall tales abounded. Nor
were popular magazine articles any help. Most stories about Gila
monsters were of a sensational nature, and the animal's role, if not
disgusting, was decidedly ominous. In Western adventure yarns and in
campfire tales, the lizard was a harbinger of suffering and death. Even
when the monster's supposed victims survived, the Gila monster's fate
was always death and destruction. When real Gila monsters could no
longer be viewed as serious villains, science fiction writers created
radiated, oversize mutants to terrorize Southwest towns in such pulp
novels as *Damnation Alley* and *Gila!*. So odious was the reptile's image
that, despite covering almost every other Southwest topic, *Arizona
Highways* magazine (where nothing bad ever happens) did not see fit to
publish a piece on the Gila monster until 1990. The poor Gila monster
was portrayed as vicious even in advertisements, some of them quite
recent (Fig. 25).

Figure 25. Ad for Nocona boots in a 1983 issue of *Playboy* magazine.

No less than three major Hollywood films have briefly featured Gila monsters, with the reptile playing the starring role in at least one grade B movie, *The Giant Gila Monster* (McLendon Studios, 1959). Riding the wave of atomic mutant pictures, this thriller's story-line involved a monster-sized *Heloderma* who terrorized trailer courts and Southwest citizens before being dispatched by a plucky teen-ager driving a nitroglycerine-laden hotrod into his belly! Enough said.

Far better known is the Gila monster in *The Treasure of the Sierra Madre* (Warner Brothers, 1948) directed by John Huston and starring Walter Huston, Humphrey Bogart, Tim Holt, and Bruce Bennett. In this classic film of human greed set in Mexico, a dramatic scene lacking in the original novel by B. Traven takes place. Near the men's gold mining camp, John Huston illustrates Dobbs' (Bogart's) growing paranoia by having Curtin (Tim Holt) spot a Gila monster crawling under a rock. Unknown to Curtin, the hole into which the Gila monster has crawled is where Dobbs has cached his share of the gold. Seeing Curtin prying up the rock to get at the Gila monster, Dobbs accuses him of wanting to steal his "goods." Curtin then challenges Dobbs to put his hand in the hole if he doesn't believe a Gila monster is in there. Dobbs, convinced that Curtin is lying, yet fearful of doing so, refuses, and a fight takes place. After overcoming Dobbs, Curtin prys up the rock and reveals the Gila monster which he promptly shoots with a pistol, leaving Dobbs to contemplate his wrongful suspicions.

In a more recent film, *Butch Cassidy and the Sundance Kid* (20th Century Fox, 1969), Utah outlaws Butch (Paul Newman) and Sundance (Robert Redford) attempt to elude a pursuing posse by taking refuge in an area of almost solid rock where their tracks will not show. Hearing a scratching movement behind them, the deadly, fast-drawing Sundance whirls around and blasts the source of the noise -- a hapless Gila monster. It's all over in a second.

You have to be even quicker than Sundance to catch the Gila monster scene toward the end of *Fat Man and Little Boy* (Paramount, 1989). Immediatley prior to the detonation of the world's first atomic bomb, a Gila monster is shown clinging to a rock in the New Mexico desert. Then the screen fades to white.

All of these movies are similar in that the Gila monster is invariably shown out of its normal range and each one meets the same fate -- being blown to pieces.

Nonetheless, the Gila monster's image was definitely on the upswing by the late 1980's. Sensational articles declined perceptibly, and what articles did appear showed the Gila monster in a more sympathetic light. Facts have became more popular than fiction, and most of the recent literature discussing Gila monsters has been of an informative nature. By the end of the decade, scientific studies of the animal's life history had been conducted at Arizona State University, the University of Arizona, and Utah State University, and the impacts of land use practices on Gila monsters had been investigated by the U. S. Bureau of Land Management and Bureau of Reclamation. That more is not known about Gila monster populations and life history is largely due to the emphasis on those species classified as threatened and endangered, such as the desert tortoise.

THE GILA MONSTER AS A SOUTHWEST SYMBOL

You have heard enough of the beauties of Arizona. Let me cool you off with one of the horrors...

Prof. George A. Treadwell, "The Gila Monster" a dinner address to the Hon. John N. Irwin, Governor of Arizona Territory, July 28, 1891

With the entry of the United States in World War I in 1917, the Arizona Militia was formed into the Arizona National Guard. The Guard adopted as its crest and epaulet insignia a Gila monster with the word *Cuidado* ("Beware") for a logo (Fig. 26). Known as the Cuidados or "Gila Monster Regiment," the unit was attached to the 40th Infantry Division out of Los Angeles, California. In 1941 the Cuidados became a separate combat divison within the 45th Infantry Divison composed of National Guard units from New Mexico, Texas, and Oklahoma as well as Arizona.

While training in Panama in 1941, the largely Mexican-American Cuidados became acutely aware of the deadly poisonous snake called the bushmaster. So impressed were the Cuidados with the bushmaster that they dropped the less ferocious Gila monster from their regimental crest and replaced the lizard with a bushmaster and a *bolo* (*machete*) insignia. After serving six years in the Pacific theater, the combat seasoned Cuidados returned to Arizona as a National Guard unit. In 1969 they attained full Divison status (the 258th), retaining the Bushmaster insignia on their new shoulder patch.

The Gila monster crest and Cuidado logo was retained, however, by the 153rd Field Artillery Battalion stationed in Glendale, Arizona. The Gila monster crest thus remains as an insignia in modified form through to the present day (Fig. 27). During Operation Desert Storm in 1991, a detachment of the Cuidados was assigned the mission of removing land mines in the Kuwaiti desert.

Figure 26. Arizona National Guard "Cuidado" Regimental crest and logo. Photo taken at the Arizona Military Museum.

Figure 27. Battalion epaulet insignia of 153rd Field Artillery, Glendale, Arizona.

It would, therefore, seem natural that when the time came for Arizona to select a state reptile that the Gila monster would be the obvious choice. Not only is the American distribution of the Gila monster largely confined to Arizona, the lizard is almost as characteristic of Arizona's Sonoran Desert as the state flower, the saguaro cactus. But the Gila monster is *not* Arizona's state reptile, and therein lies a tale.

By 1985, Arizona already had a state bird, the cactus wren; a state mammal, the ring-tailed cat; and a state tree, the paloverde. The Education and Nongame branches of the Arizona Game and Fish Department now decided that Arizona should also have a state reptile, a state amphibian, and a state fish. Three animals in each category were selected by the Department's new Nongame Branch for a vote by grade school students. The winning reptile, amphibian, and fish would then be included in a bill giving these species official state status.

The Game Department's candidates for state reptile were the Gila monster, desert tortoise, and Arizona ridge-nosed rattlesnake. When the school kids cast their votes, the results were natural but unexpected. The Arizona trout beat out the Colorado River squawfish and hump-backed chub for state fish. Among the amphibians, the Arizona tree-frog was selected over the Colorado River toad and red-spotted toad. The Arizona ridge-nosed rattlesnake, a local subspecies of a small rattler found primarily in Mexico and occurring only in three mountain ranges in Arizona, was picked as Arizona's official reptile. Since the students had been asked to decide which of the animals best represented Arizona, they had naturally chosen the animals with Arizona in their name. The legislature, after some derisive comments, approved the list as submitted. Neither they nor the Game Department were willing to face the opprobrium of negating the election by thousands of grade-schoolers.

Its lack of official recognition notwithstanding, the Gila monster now enjoys the benefits of a regional totem with a benign, although somewhat pugnacious image. A popular children's book introduces kids to the Southwest with the prospect of Gila monsters and horned toads meeting them at the airport. It is the only reptile included as a symbol in a Southwest zodiac published by the *Arizona Republic* in Phoenix ("Gila monsters are intensely loyal,") (Fig. 28). High school teams in Gila Bend, Arizona, are the "Gila Monsters" (Fig. 29), as are athletes at Eastern Arizona College in Pima (Fig. 30). To show our growing appreciation of the animal and his desert home, the Gila monster has been featured as an object d'art on tee-shirts promoting natural history institutions, on posters advertising cultural events, on Southwest greeting cards and stationery, on postcards and license plates, and on locally-made curios and jewelry (Fig. 31). One wonders when Gila monster-shaped hot air balloons and *piñatas* will make an appearance.

GILA MONSTER
(1943, 1955, 1967, 1979)

Intensely loyal, you think everything is better in New England, which has real seasons. Stand up for your beliefs, even when no one will car-pool with you. Native Arizonans born under this sign move to California. You and Burro are too alike to be compatible; choose Roadrunner.

ROADRUNNER
(1942, 1954, 1966, 1978, 1990)

You were on your way to California to be in the movies when you ran out of money. You play Scarlet O'Hara at Bobby McGee's, and love to sing at weddings. Gila Monster finds you intriguing.

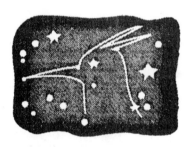

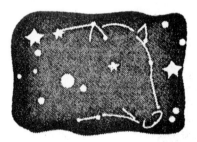

JAVELINA
(1941, 1953, 1965, 1977, 1989)

You are generous and outgoing, and have season tickets to everything. Your MasterCard is often over its limit. Odds are 5-to-2 you were born in Pennsylvania. You are compatible with Bull.

Figure 28. Southwest zodiac symbols, including the Gila monster. *Arizona Republic* newspaper, Phoenix.

Figure 29. Gila Bend High School's Gila monster logo on gymnasium wall.

Figure 30. Eastern Arizona College's Gila monster logo created by cartoonist Reg Manning.

Figure 31. Elaine Brown and collection of Gila monster "miscellanea."

The Gila monster is also wonderfully useful for spicing up the regional idiom. The hyperbole of "hanging on like a Gila monster" is a not infrequently used Southwest metaphor, and fishermen brag that the "bass were so big that we used Gila monsters for bait." A recluse, arrested for poaching deer and rustling livestock in New Mexico's Gila Wilderness, called himself the "Gila Monster" and claimed that he learned to talk to the lizards when living in Sonora, Mexico. And a popular "Tour of the Gila" bicycle event through New Mexico's Gila National Forest near Silver City features a 110-mile road race that is so arduous it's termed the "Gila *Monster*." (Fig. 32)

Today, the Gila monster is celebrated for what he is: a unique, native Southwesterner whose infrequent appearances bestow a special blessing to the land and brighten any day afield. The animal's venomous nature is considered fascinating rather than sinister, and his bizarre reputation is regarded more as charming regional folklore than the product of Gothic nightmares. As one of the most brillianty colored, yet least seen and understood inhabitants of the Sonoran Desert, the lizard has come to symbolize the desert's beauty and mystery. Let us hope that the Gila monster will remain a source of such inspiration and be with us always.

Figure 32. Gila monsters, based on the ancient Mimbres design, from a "Tour of the Gila" bicycle race promotional. Art by Marilyn Gendron.

REFERENCES

There is more nonsense in the scientific and medical literature on the Gila monster than on all other venomous reptiles in Arizona combined.

C. H. Lowe, C. R. Schwalbe, and T. B. Johnson,
The Venomous Reptiles of Arizona, 1986

The following is a bibliography of books, scientific articles, scholarly theses, government reports, and popular magazine accounts consulted in our review of the literature on Gila monsters and their habitat. The list does not include the newspaper articles and films cited in the text.

BOOKS AND BULLETINS

Anonymous. 1953. American wild life illustrated. William H. Wise and Co., New York. 625p.

Arnold, O. and M. E. Cason. 1940. Desert plants and animals. Arizona Printers Inc. 93p.

Attenborough, D. 1984. The Living Planet. Little, Brown & Co., Boston.

Bahr, D. M., J. Gregorio, D. I. Lopez and A. Alvarez. 1974. Piman shamanism and staying sickness. Univ. Arizona Press, Tucson. 332p.

Baird, S. F. 1859. Reptiles of the Boundary. pp. 1-35 *In* United States and Mexican Boundary survey under the order of Lieutenant Colonel W. H. Emory. Vol. 3, Pt. 2, U. S. Dept. of the Int., Wash., D. C.

Barbour, T. 1926. Reptiles and amphibians, their habits and adaptations (revised ed.). Houghton Mifflin Co., Boston and New York. 129p.

Beddard, F. E. 1905. Natural history in zoological gardens. Lippincot, Philadelphia, PA. 310p.

Behler, J. L. and F. W. King. 1979. The Audubon Society field guide to North American reptiles and amphibians. Alfred A. Knopf, New York. 719p.

Bellairs, A. 1970. The life of reptiles. Universe books, New York.

Benson, L. and R. A. Darrow. 1981. Trees and shrubs of the southwestern deserts. Univ. of Arizona Press, Tucson. 416p.

Bogart, C. M. and M. R. Del Campo. 1956. The Gila Monster and its allies: The relationships, habits and behavior of the lizards of the family Helodermatidae. Amer. Mus. Nat. Hist. Bull. 109. 238p.

Breen, J. F. 1974. The Encyclopedia of Reptiles and Amphibians. TFH Publications Ltd.

Brown, D. E. (ed.). 1982. The biotic communities of the American Southwest - U. S. and Mexico. Desert Plants 4 (1--4):1-342.

REFERENCES

Buckley, E. E. and N. Porges, eds. Venoms. Amer. Assoc. Advance. Sci., Washington, D. C. Publ. 44:1-467.

Campbell, J. A. and W. W. Lamar. 1989. The venomous reptiles of Latin America. Comstock Publishing Assoc. (Cornell Univ. Press). Ithaca, NY and London. 425p.

Capula, M. Simon & Schuster's Guide to Reptiles and Amphibians of the World. Simon & Schuster, New York.

Cochran, D. M. 1944. Dangerous reptiles. Smithsonian Publ. 3753: 275-324.

Coues, E. 1875. Synopsis of the reptilels and batrachians of Arizona. *In* Report upon geographical and geological explorations and surveys west of the 100th Meridian, in charge of First Lt. Geo. M. Wheeler. Vol. 5, Zoology, pp. 585-633. G.P.O., Wash. D. C.

Dannaldson, J. A. 1937. Pp. 43-46 *In* Serpent trails. Kellaway-Ide Co., Los Angeles.

Ditmars, R. L. 1933 (2nd ed.). Reptiles of the world. Macmillan, New York. 321p.

_____. 1945. The reptiles of North America. Doubleday and Doran and Co., Garden City, NY. 476p.

Dodge, N. N. 1964. Poisonous dwellers of the desert. Southwest. Mon. Assoc. Pop. Series No. 3:1-44.

Felger, R. S. and N. B. Moser. 1985. People of the desert and sea: ethnobotany of the Seri Indians. Univ. of Arizona Press, Tucson. 435p.

Gilmore, C. W. 1928. The fossil lizards of North America. Mem. National Acad. Sci. 22:1-201.

Gorsuch, D. M. 1934. Life history of the Gambel's quail in Arizona. Univ. of Arizona Bull. 2:1-89.

Gustafson, A. M., (ed.) 1966. John Spring's Arizona. Univ. of Arizona Press, Tucson. 326p.

Grismek, H. C. Bernhard. 1984. Grizmek's Animal Life Encyclopedia, Volume 6, Reptiles. Van Nostrand Reinhold Company, New York.

Halliday, T. and K. Adler. 1986. The Encyclopedia of Reptiles and Amphibians. Equinox Ltd.

Heintzelman, S. P. 1858-1859. Journal. *In* North, D. M. T., 1890. Samuel Peter Heintzelman and the Sonora Exploring and Mining Company. Univ. Arizona Press, Tucson. 248p.

Heyman, M. M. 1975. Reptiles and amphibians of the American southwest. Doubleshoe Publ., Scottsdale, AZ. 77 p.

Hinton, R. J. 1878. The hand-book to Arizona. Payot, Upham, San Francisco. 431p.

Hylander, C. J. 1954. Animals in armor. MacMillan Co., New York. 203p.

James, G. W. 1906. The wonders of the Colorado Desert. Vol. I. Boston.

Kauffeld, C. 1957. Snakes and Snake Hunting. Hanover House.

_____. 1969. Snakes: The Keeper and The Kept. Doubleday & Co., Garden City, NY.

Killian, J. L. 1954. Common reptiles of Arizona. Ariz. Game and Fish Dept., Phoenix. 16p.

Klots, A. B. 1954. Desert life. Nelson Doubleday Inc., Garden City, NY. 62p.

Laird, C. 1976. The Chemehuevis. Malki Museum Press, Banning, CA. 349p.

Lawler, H. E. and W. K. Wintin. 1987. Captive management and propagation of the reticulated Gila monster *Heloderma suspectum suspectum* Cope. Pp. 48-56. *In* Captive propogation and husbandry of reptiles and amphibians. R. Gowen, ed. North. California Herpetological Soc. Spec. Publ. 4.

Loeb, L., C. L. Alsberg, E. Cooke, E. P. Corson-White, M. S. Fleisher, H. Fox, T. S. Githens, S. Leopold, M. K. Meyers, M. E. Rehfuss, D. Rivas and L. Tuttle. 1913. The venom of *Heloderma*. Carnegie Inst. Washington Publ. No. 177:1-244.

Loveridge, A. 1946. Reptiles of the Pacific world. Macmillan, New York. 259p.

Lowe, C. H., Jr., C. R. Schwalbe, and T. B. Johnson. 1986. The venemous reptiles of Arizona. Arizona Game and Fish Dept., Phoenix. 115p.

Mauldin, B. 1949. [Notes on the Gila monster]. Pp. 157- 159. *In* A sort of a saga. William Sloane Assoc., New York.

McCollough, N. C. and J. F. Gennaro. 1971. Treatment of venomous snakebite in the United States. Pp. 137-154 *In* Snake venoms and envenomation. S. A. Minton, ed. Marcel Dekker, Inc., New York. 188p.

Nentvig, S. J. 1980. Rudo Ensayo: a description of Sonora and Arizona in 1764. Translated, clarified and annotated by A. F. Pradeau and R. R. Rasmussen. Univ. of Arizona Press, Tucson. 160p.

Obst, J., K. Richter, and U. Jacob. 1988. The Completely Illustrated Atlas of Reptiles and Amphibians for the Terrarium. TFH Publications.

Pfefferkorn, I., S.J. 1949. Sonora: a description of the Province. Univ. of New Mexico Press, Albuquerque. 329p.

Pope, C. H. 1955. The Reptile World. Alfred A. Knopf, New York.

Quebbeman, F. E. 1966. Medicine in Territorial Arizona. Arizona Hist. Found., Phoenix. 424p.

Romer, A. S. 1956. The osteology of the reptiles. Univ. of Chicago Press. 772 p.

Russell, F. 1908. The Pima Indians. Pp. 264, 307-308 *In* Twenty-sixth Annual Report of the Bureau of American Ethnology, 1904-1905. W. H. Holmes, Chief. U. S. G.P.O., Washington, D. C. 512 p.

Russell, F. E. 1983. Snake venom poisoning. Chapter 9: Gila monster (*Heloderma suspectum*). Scholium Intern., Great Neck, NY. pp.395-419.

Saxton, D., L. Saxton, and S. Enos. 1983. Dictionary Papago/Pima - English, O'othham - Mil-gahn; English - Papago/Pima, Mil-gahn - O'othham. 2nd ed. R. L. Cherry, (ed.). Univ. of Arizona Press, Tucson. 145p.

Sharmat, M. W. 1980. Gila monsters meet you at the airport. Macmillan Publ. Co. Inc., New York.

Schmidt, K. P. and R. F. Inger. 1957. Living Reptiles of The World. Doubleday & Co., Inc., Garden City, NY.

Shannon, F. A. 1956. Comments on the treatment of reptile poisoning. Pp. 405-412 *In* Venoms. E. E. Buckley and N. Porges, eds. Amer. Assoc. Advance. Sci., Wash. D. C.

Simons, L. 1981. Gila! New American Library, New York. 166p.

Smith, H. M. 1946. Handbook of lizards. Cornell Univ. Press, Ithaca, NY and London. Reprinted in 1971 by Comstock Publ. Assoc. 557p.

Smith, H. M. and E. D. Brodie Jr. 1982. A Guide to field Identification of Reptiles and Amphibians of North America. Golden Press, New York.

Smith, L. L., and R. W. Doughty. 1984. The amazing armadillo: geography of a folk critter. Univ. of Texas Press, Austin. 134p.

Smith, R. L. 1982. Venomous animals of Arizona. Univ. of Arizona Coop. Ext. Serv., Tucson. 134p.

Spring, J. 1966. John Spring's Arizona. A. M. Gustafson, ed. Univ. Arizona Press, Tucson. 326p.

Stahnke, H. L. 1966. The treatment of venomous bites and stings. Revised ed. Arizona State Univ., Tempe. 117p.

Stebbins, R. C. 1985. A field guide to Western reptiles and amphibians. Peterson Field Guide Series No. 16, Houghton Mifflin Co., Boston. 336p.

Switak, Karl H. 1984. The Life of Desert Reptiles and Amphibians. Karl H. Switak.

Tanara, M. U. 1978. The World of Amphibians and Reptiles. Gallery Books.

Tinkham, E. R. 1956. The deadly nature of Gila monster venom. Pp. 59-63 *In* Venoms. E. E. Buckley and N. Porges, eds. Amer. Assoc. Advance. Sci., Wash., D. C.

_____. 1971. The biology of the Gila Monster. Pp. 387-413 *In* Venomous animals and their venoms: Vol. 2, Venomous vertebrates. W. Bücherl and E. E. Buckley, eds. Academic Press, New York.

Tyler, A. 1956. An auto-antivenin in the Gila monster and its relation to a concept of natural auto-antibodies. Pp. 65-74 *In* Venoms, E. E. Buckley and N. Porges, eds. Amer. Assoc. Advanc. Sci., Wash., D. C.

Underhill, R. M. 1946. Papago Indian religion. Columbia Univ. Press Contrib. to Anthopology No. 33:1-359.

Van Denburgh, J. 1897. The reptiles of the Pacific Coast and Great Basin, an account of the species known to inhabit California, Oregon, Washington, Idaho and Nevada. Occas. Papers Calif. Acad. Sci. 5:1-236.

Van Denburgh, J. 1922. The reptiles of western North America. Occas. Papers California Acad. Sci. 10:1- 611.

Vogel, Z. 1964. Reptiles and amphibians: their care and behavior. Viking Press, New York. 228p.

Vorhies, C. T. 1917. Poisonous animals of the desert. Univ. of Ariz. Agr. Expt. Sta. Bull. 83:357-392.

_____. 1936. Important reptiles. *In* Arizona and its heritage. Univ. of Arizona Bull. 3:1-291.

Woodbury, A. M. 1931. A descriptive catalog of the reptiles of Utah. Bull. Univ. Utah 21(5):1-129.

Wright, H. B. 1929. Long ago told. D. Appleton, New York. 290p.

Wynne, R. H. 1981. Lizards in Captivity. TFH Publications, Ltd.

Yarrow, H. C. 1875. Report upon the collections of batrachians and reptiles made in portions of Nevada, Utah, California, Colorado, New Mexico, and Arizona during the years 1871, 1872, 1873, and 1874. Pp. 509-585 *In* Wheeler, G. M. Report upon geographical and geological explorations and surveys west of the one hundredth meridian. Vol. V. Zoology. Gov. Print. Office, Wash., D. C.

Wild, P. 1986. The saguaro forest. Northland Press, Flagstaff, AZ. 65p.

Zelazny, R. 1969. Damnation alley. Berkley Publ. Corp., New York. 157p.

Zim, H. S. and H. M. Smith. 1953. Reptiles and amphibians: a guide to familiar American species. Simon and Schuster, New York. 160p.

MAGAZINE AND JOURNAL ARTICLES

Adamson, S. 1986. The desert monster. Explorer 28(1):26-28.

Aker, J. W. 1949. The Gila monster. The Arizona Times (Phoenix). Mar. 12:14.

Allen, M. J. 1933. Report on a collection of amphibians and reptiles from Sonora, Mexico, with the description of a new lizard. Occas. Papers Mus. Zool. Univ. Mich. 259:1-15.

Anonymous. 1879. The Gila monster. Sci. Amer. 41(25):399.

_____. 1882. [Note on the toxic nature of *Heloderma* venom]. Amer. Naturalist 16::842.

_____. 1882a. Illustrations of new or rare animals in the Zoological Society's living collection. The Sonoran heloderm (*Heloderma suspectum*). Nature 27:153-154.

_____. 1890. Gila monster (*Heloderma horridus*). Homeopathic Recorder, 5:163-69.

_____. 1891. The Gila monster. Amer. Naturalist 25:688.

_____. 1891. The effects of *Heloderma* poison. J. Homoeopathics 5:45.

_____. 1893. A Gila monster's bite. Terrible fate of a tourist's companion in Arizona. Homoeopathic Recorder. 8:318-320.

_____. 1894. The therapeutic value of *Heloderma* venom and a discussion of dosage and caution that should be observed in use of venom from "*Heloderma hor*". Homeopathic Recorder. 9:141, 506.

_____. 1943. Gila monster made poor bosom pet. Scenic Southwest 15(Mar.):2,3, 5.

—————. 1954. It probably tickled. Calif. Acad. Sci. News Letter 180:1-4.

—————. 1956. Is whiskey a cure for snakebite? Arizona Beverage J. Aug.:8.

—————. 1971. Success with Gila monsters. Zoonooz 44(2):12.

Arnberger, L. P. 1948. Gila monster swallows quail eggs whole. Herpetologica 4:209-210.

Arrington, O. N. 1930. Notes on the two poisonous lizards with special reference to *Heloderma suspectum*. Bull. Antivenin Inst. Amer. 4(2):29-35.

A. W. 1917. Lewis Lindsay Dyche. Auk 34:116.

Barrett, S. L. and J. A. Humphrey. 1986. Agonistic interactions between *Gopherus agassizii* (Testudinidae) and *Heloderma suspectum* (Helodermatidae). Southwest. Naturalist. 31:262-263.

Beck, C. 1980. Gila monster hatches at Memphis Zoo. AAZPA Newsletter. 21(1):14.

Beck, D. D. 1985. *Heloderma suspectum cinctum* (banded Gila monster). Pattern/coloration. Herpetological Rev. 16:53.

—————. 1990. Ecology and behavior of the Gila monster in southwestern Utah. J. Herpetology. 24:54-68.

Beddard, F. E. 1906. On the vascular system of *Heloderma*, with notes on that of the monitors and crocodiles. Proc. Zool. Soc. London:601-625.

Bell, J. G. 1932. A log of the Texas-California cattle trail. J. E. Haley, ed. Southwest. Hist. Quart. 36:47-66.

Bendire, C. E. 1887. Whip scorpion and the Gila monster. Forest and Stream. 29:64-65.

Benes, E. S. 1968. A study in laboratory maintenance of the Gila monster. Lab. Animal Care. 18(1):69-74.

Bicket, J. C. 1982. *Heloderma suspectum cinctum*. Herpetological Rev. 13:131.

Bloyd, G. R. 1970. The Gila monster (*Heloderma suspectum*). Bull. Florissant Herpetological Soc. 8:1-2.

Bogert, C. M. 1930. Saurians of the Southwest. Nature Mag. 16:356-359.

—————. 1939. Reptiles under the sun. Natural Hist. 44:26-37.

—————. 1948. Gila monster. Natural Hist. 10:434.

—————. 1956. The world's only venomous lizards. Animal Kingdom 56:105-109.

—————. 1959. The Gila monster. Audubon Mag. 61(4):160-163.

—————. 1959. How reptiles regulate their body temperature. Sci. Amer. 210(4):105-120.

Bogert, C. M. and J. A. Oliver. 1945. A preliminary analysis of the herpetofauna of Sonora. Bull. Amer. Mus. Nat. Hist. 83(6):297-426.

Boocock, R. 1893a *Heloderma horridus*. Notes on proving. Homoeopathic Recorder. 8:97-103.

—————. 1893b. Proving of *Heloderma horridus*. The Gila monster. Homoeopathic Recorder. 8:145-163.

_____. 1894a. [Letter expressing hope to gain renown through experiments with *Heloderma horridus*] Homoeopathic Recorder. 9:550-551.

_____. 1894b. *Heloderma horridus* in heart failure and paralysis of the lungs. Homoeopathic Recorder. 9:628-630.

Boulenger, G. A. 1882. [Observations made on *Heloderma*.] Proc. Zool. Soc. London: 631-632.

_____. 1891a. Notes on the osteology of *Heloderma horridum* and *Heloderma suspectum*, with remarks on the systematic position of the Helodermatidae and on the vertebrae of the Lacertilia. Proc. Zool. Soc. London. 109-118.

_____. 1891b. The anatomy of *Heloderma*. Nature 44:444.

Bowler, J. K. 1977. Longevity of reptiles and amphibians in North American collections. Soc. for the Study of Amphibians and Reptiles. Misc. Publ. Herpetol. Cir. 6:1-32.

Boynton, K. L. 1971. The Gila monster. Desert Mag. 34(Nov.):18-21.

Bradford, T. L. 1895. Is the Gila monster venomous? Homoeopathic Recorder. 10:1-13.

Bradley, W. G. and J. E. Deacon. 1966. Distribution of the Gila monster in the northern Mojave Desert. Copeia 1966: 365-366.

Brattstrom, B. H. 1954. Amphibians and reptiles from Gypsum Cave, Nevada. Bull. So. Calif. Acad. Sci. 53:8-12.

Brennan, G. A. 1924. A case of death from *Heloderma* bite. Copeia 1924:45.

Brimley, C. S. 1905. Notes on the food and feeding habits of some American reptiles. J. Mitchell Sci. Soc. 21:149-155.

Brown, P. C. 1889. The Gila monster. The Great Divide 1:31.

Brown, W. H. and C. H. Lowe, Jr. 1954. Physiological effects of labial gland secretion from *Heloderma* (Gila monster) upon *Heloderma*. Amer. J. Physiol. 177(3): 539-540.

_____. 1955. Technique for obtaining maximum yields of fresh labial gland secretions from the lizard *Heloderma suspectum*. Copeia 1955:63.

Cahoon, J. C. 1887. The Gila Monster (letter to the editor). Forest and Stream. 29 (Nov. 3):283.

Campbell, H. 1976. New Mexico's endangered monster. New Mexico Wildlife. 21(4):25-30.

Cameron, H. A. 1898. *Heloderma horridum (suspectum)*. J. Homoeopathics, Philadelphia 1:295-306.

Campbell, J. A. and J. P. Vannini. 1988. A new subspecies of beaded lizard, *Heloderma horridum*, from the Motagua Valley of Guatemala. J. Herpetol. 22:457-468.

Cheeks, L. W. 1990. Watch out! The little monsters bite. Ariz. Highways. (Aug.):42-45.

Clarke, W. B. 1890. The Gila monster. Medical Curr. 6:373-376.

Conant, R. and R. G. Hudson. 1949. Longevity records for reptiles and amphibians in the Philadelphia Zoological Garden. Herpetologica 5:1-8.

Cooke, E. and L. Loeb. 1908. Haemolytic action of the venom of *Heloderma suspectum*. Proc. Soc. Exp. Biol. Med. 5:104-105.

Cooper, W. E., jr. 1989. Prey odor discrimination in the Varanoid lizards *Heloderma suspectum* and *Varanus exanthematicus*. Ethology 81:250-258.

Cope, E. D. 1866. On the Reptilia and Batrachia of the Sonoran province of the Nearctic region. Proc. Acad. Nat. Sci. Philadelphia 18:300-314.

_____. 1869. [On *Heloderma suspectum*.] Proc. Acad. Nat. Sci. Philadelphia 21:4-5.

_____. 1882. Note on the preceding paper [R. W. Shufeldt, 1882, The bite of the Gila monster (*Heloderma suspectum*)]. Amer. Naturalist 16:908-909.

Cowles, R. B. and C. M. Bogert. 1936. The herpetology of the Boulder Dam region (NV, AZ, UT). Herpetologica 1:33-42.

Crosman, A. M. 1956. A longevity record for Gila monster. Copeia 1956:54.

Cross, J. K., and M. S. Rand. 1979. Climbing activity in wild-ranging Gila monsters *Heloderma suspectum* (Helodermatidae). Southwest. Naturalist 24:703-705.

Curtis, L. 1949. Notes on the eggs of *Heloderma horridum*. Herpetologica 5:148.

Curtis, M., D. Waldron, H. Calderwood, and E. Jacobson. 1980. Repair of abdominal hernia in a gila monster (*Heloderma suspectum*). Veterinary Med./Small Animal Clinician. June:1050-52.

Demeter, B. J. 1986. Combat behavior in the Gila monster (*Heloderma suspectum cinctum*). Herp. Rev. 17:9-11.

DeVries, J. 1969. Opinions differ on L-C method in the treatment of snake bite. Arizona Republic, Phoenix. Apr. 22.

Dixon, J. R., and P. A. Medica. 1965. Noteworthy records of reptiles from New Mexico. Herpetologica 21:72-75.

Douglas, E. 1910. The Gila monster - a convicted suspect. Ariz. Mag. 1(Dec):9-10.

Duelman, W. E. 1950. A case of *Heloderma* poisoning. Copeia 1950:151.

Durham, F. E. 1951. Observations on a captive Gila monster. Amer. Midl. Natuarlist 45:460-470.

Editor, 1899. Concerning the "Gila monster". The Arizona Graphic. 1(Sept.):9.

Edwards, C. L. 1924. The Gila monster. Nature Mag. 4:26,30.

Edwards, H. T., and D. B. Dill. 1935. Properties of reptilian blood. II, the Gila monster (*Heloderma suspectum* Cope). J. Cell. and Comp. Physiol. 6(1):21-35.

Emery, J. A., and F. E. Russell. 1961. Studies with cooling measures following injection of *Crotalus* venom. Copeia 3:323-325.

Englehardt, G. P. 1914. Notes on the Gila monster. Copeia 1914:1-2.

English, P. F. 1927. Notes on *Heloderma suspectum* and *Iguana tuberculata*. Science 66:37.

Fast, J. E., and L. R. Caywood. 1936, re-issued 1952. Life figures on Hohokam pottery. U. S. D. I. National Park Serv. Southwest. Nat. Mon. Spec. Rep. 2:1-4 + plates.

Fayer, J. 1882. [On the Heloderma.] Proc. Zool. Soc. of London: 632.

Ford, R. S. 1981. *Heloderma suspectum cinctum*. Herp. Rev. 12(2):64.

Funk, R. S. 1966. Notes about *Heloderma suspectum* along the western extremity of its range. Herpetologica 22: 254-258.

Garman, S. W. "1890" (1891). The "Gila monster". Bull. Essex Inst. 22(4-6):60-69.

Gates, G. O. 1955. Mating habits of the Gila Monster. Herpetologica 12:184.

Gloyd, H. K. 1937. A herpetological consideration of faunal areas in southern Arizona. Bull. Chicago Acad. Sci. 5:79-136.

G.N.K. 1887. The Gila monster [letter to the editor]. 29 (Aug. 25):86.

Goodfellow, G. 1907. The Gila monster again [letter to the editor]. Scientific Amer. 96 (Mar. 30):271.

Gordon, G. 1934. Fiends of the desert. Popular Sci. Monthly. Nov.:30-31.

Gorsuch, D. 1937. Gila monster bites dog. Arizona Mag. 1 (June):14

Grant, C. 1952. Probably the first legislation to protect a poisonous animal. Herpetologica 8:64.

Grant, M. L. , and L. J. Henderson. 1957. A case of Gila monster poisoning with a summary of some previous accounts. Proc. Iowa Acad. Sci. 64:686-697

Haddon, E. P. 1954. Little monster. Outdoor Life 114 46- 49.

Haddon, E. P. and M. Branham. 1958. Duel in the dunes. Desert Mag. 21(Dec.):8-9.

Hardy, L. M. and R. W. McDiarmid. 1969. The Amphibians and Reptiles of Sinaloa, Mexico. University of Kansas. 18(3):39-252.

Haury, E. W. 1967. The Hohokam, first masters of the American desert. National Geographic. May.

Heath, W. G. 1961. A trailing device for small animals designed for field study of the Gila monster (*Heloderma suspectum*). Copeia 1961:491-492.

Hensley, M. M. 1949. Mammal diet of *Heloderma* Herpetologica 5:152.

_____. 1950. Notes on the natural history of *Heloderma suspectum*. Trans. Kansas Acad. Sci. 53:268- 269.

Holm, J. F. 1897. Some notes on the histology of the poison glands of *Heloderma suspectum*. Anat. Ariz. 13:80.

Housholder, V. 1965. Arizona's poisonous reptiles: The Gilá monster. Ariz. Wildl. Sportsman 36(6):26-27.

Huey, L. M. 1942. A vertebrate faunal survey of the Organ Pipe Cactus National Monument, Arizona. Trans. San Diego Soc. Natural Hist. 9:353-376.

Hull, P. 1899. Concerning the "Gila monster". Ariz. Graphic 1(2):9

Irwin, B.I.D. 1859. Report. In J. E.Serven, 1965. The Military Posts of Sonoita Creek. Smoke Signal. 12:1- 24.

Jackson, E. 1941. As tough as they come. Region 3 Quart., U. S. Nat. Park Serv. 3(2):2-9.

Jennings, M. R. 1984. Longevity records for lizards of the Family Helodermatidae. Bull. Maryland Herpetol. Soc. 20 (1): 22-23.

John-Alder, H., C. H. Lowe and A. F. Bennett. 1983. Thermal dependence of locomotor energetics and aerobic capacity of the Gila monster (*Heloderma suspectum*). J. Comparative Physiol. 151:119-126.

Johnson, B. D., J. C. Tullar, and H. L. Stahnke. 1966. A quantitative protozoan bio-assay method for determining venom potencies. Toxicon 3:297.

Jones, K. B. 1983. Movement patterns and foraging ecology of Gila monsters (*Heloderma* suspectum Cope) in northwestern Arizona. Herpetologica 39:247-253.

Kauffeld, C. F. 1943. Field notes on some Arizona reptiles and amphibians. Amer. Midl. Naturalist 29(2):342-359.

_____. 1949. Arizona adventure. In Animaland, Staten Island Zool. Soc. 16(6):3p.

_____. 1954. Gila monster. In Animaland, Staten Island Zool. Soc. 21(5):4p.

Kimball, T. 1951. Game and Fish Department doings. Ariz. Wildl. Sportsman. Aug.:33.

King, F. W. 1932. Herpetological records and notes from the vicinity of Tucson, Arizona, July and August 1930. Copeia 1932: 175-177.

_____. 1974. International trade and endangered species. Intern. Zoo Yearbook 14:2-13.

Koster, W. J. 1951. The distribution of the Gila monster in New Mexico. Herpetologica 7:97-101.

Larsen, W., R. Lunt, and P. Rippee. 1969. The brachycardia reflex in the Gila monster. Proc. Utah Acad. Sci. Arts Lett. 46(2):131-132.

Lilienthal, "Dr." 1894. *Heloderma*. Homeopathic Recorder. 9:495-498.

Limbacher, H. P. and C. H. Lowe, Jr. 1959. The treatment of poisonous bites and stings. Arizona Med. 16:490- 495.

Linsdale, J. M. 1940. Amphibians and reptiles in Nevada. Proc. Amer. Acad. Arts and Sci. 73(8):197-257.

Little, E. L., Jr. 1940. Amphibians and reptiles of the Roosevelt Reservoir area, Arizona. Copeia 1940:260- 265.

Lockington, W. N. 1879. Notes on some reptiles and Batrachia of the Pacific Coast. Amer. Naturalist 13:780-783.

_____. 1879a. *Heloderma suspectum* Cope. Amer. Naturalist 13:781-782.

_____. 1879b. Notes on some reptiles and Batrachia of the Pacific Coast. Amer. Naturalist 14:780-783.

Loeb, L. 1921. The venom of Heloderma. J. Amer. Mus. Natural Hist. 21:93-95.

Loeb, L. and M. S. Fleisher. 1910. The absorption of the venom of *Heloderma suspectum*. Proc. Soc. Exp. Biol. Med. 7:91-93.

Lowe, C. H., Jr. and H. P. Limbacher. 1961. The treatment of poisonous bites and stings: II. Arizona coral snake and Gila monster bite. Ariz. Med. 18:128-131.

"M.", H. 1907. The bite of the Gila monster. Scientific Amer. 96:251.

Martin, C. J. 1914. Lizard venom. Nature 93:123.

M[artin], H. N. 1883. The physiological action of *Heloderma* poison. Science 1:372.

Mebs, D. 1968. Some studies on the biochemistry of the venom gland of *Heloderma horridum*. Toxicon. 5(3):225- 226.

Mitchell, S. W. and E. T. Reichert. 1883. A partial study of the poison of *Heloderma suspectum* Cope, the Gila monster. Science 1:373.

Mitchell, S. W. and E. T. Reichert. 1883. A partial study of the poison of *Heloderma suspectum* (Cope). Med. News 42:209-212.

McCollough, N. C., and J. F. Gennaro. 1963. Evaluation of venomous snake bite in the southern United States... J. Florida Med. Assoc. 49:959-967.

Moore, H. R. 1958. Our vanishing miniature monsters. Arizona Days and Ways Mag. (Ariz. Republic). Jan. 19:50-51.

_____. 1959. Gila monster -- Boris Karloff of the desert. Arizona Days and Ways Mag. (Arizona Republic) Nov.22:36-39.

Mulch, E. 1952. Why protect gila monsters? Ariz. Wildl. Sportsman. Sept.:30-31, 71.

M.Y.B. 1894. The Gila monster [letter to the editor]. Scientific Amer. Aug. 25:119.

Neill, W. T. 1967. The Gila monsters. Golden West 3(6):8, 55-56.

Ortenberger, R. D. 1924. Notes on the Gila monster. Proc. Okla. Acad. Sci. 4:22.

Ortenberger, A. I., and R. D. Ortenberger. 1926. Field observations on some amphibians and reptiles of Pima County, Arizona. Proc. Okla. Acad. Sci. 6: 101-121.

Osborne, S. 1983. Reticulated Gila monsters. Zoosounds. Oct.:14.

Ottley, J. R. 1981. *Heloderma suspectum suspectum*. Herp. Rev. 12:65.

Patterson, R. A. 1967a. Some physiological effects caused by venom from the Gila monster, *Heloderma suspectum*. Toxicon 5:5-10.

_____. 1967b. Smooth muscle stimulating action of venom from the Gila monster, *Heloderma suspectum*. Toxicon 5:11.

Patterson, R. A. and I. S. Lee. 1969. Effects of *Heloderma suspectum* venom on blood coagulation. Toxicon. 7:321-324.

Peterson, K. H. 1982. Reproduction in captive *Heloderma suspectum*. Herpetological Rev. 13:122-124.

Pianka, E. R. 1966. Convexity, desert lizards, and spacial heterogeneity. Ecology 47:1055-1059.

Patterson, R. A. and I. S. Lee. 1969. Effects of *Heloderma suspectum* venom on blood coagulation. Toxicon. 7:321-324.

Peterson, K. H. 1982. Reproduction in captive *Heloderma suspectum*. Herpetological Rev. 13:122-124.

Pianka, E. R. 1966. Convexity, desert lizards, and spacial heterogeneity. Ecology 47:1055-1059.

_____. 1967. On lizard species diversity: North American flatland deserts. Ecology 48:333-351.

Poston, C. D. 1885. [letter to the editor]. Forest and Stream 24:406.

Pregill, G. K., J. A. Gauthier and H. W. Greene. 1986. The evolution of helodermatid squamates, with description of a new taxon and an overview of Varanoidea. Trans. San Diego Soc. Natural Hist. 21(11):167-202.

Reed, A. C. 1953. Arizona's venom man. Arizona Highways. 29(Feb.): 28-35.

Russell, F. E., et al. 1966. Snakebite. J. Amer. Med. Assoc. 195:188.

Russell, F. E., and C. M. Bogert. 1981. Gila Monster: Its biology, venom, and bite - a review. Toxicon 19:341-359.

Ruthven, A. G. 1907. A collection of reptiles and amphibians from southern New Mexico and Arizona. Bull. Amer. Mus. Natural Hist. 23:483-603.

Schufeldt, R. W. 1882. The bite of the Gila monster (*Heloderma suspectum*). Amer. Naturalist 16:907-908.

_____. 1883. The bite of the Gila monster, *Heloderma suspectum*. J. Amer. Nat. 16:907.

_____. 1887. The Gila monster. Forest and Stream 29:24.

_____. 1890. Contributions to the study of *Heloderma suspectum*. Proc. Zool. Soc. London, 14- 18:131-132, 148-244.

_____. 1891. Some opinions on the bite of the Gila monster (*Heloderma suspectum*). Nature's Realm 2:125-129.

_____. 1891a. The poison apparatus of the *Heloderma*. Nature 43: 514-515.

_____. 1891b. Further notes on the anatomy of *Heloderma*. Nature 44:294-295.

_____. 1891c. Medical and other opinions upon the poisonous nature of the *Heloderma*. New York Medical J. May: 581-584.

_____. 1901. Hobnobbing with a Gila monster J. Homeopathics 5:42-45.

Schwartzmann, J. L., and R. D. Ohmart. 1976. Preliminary field investigations of the movements, burrow usages and body temperatures of Gila monsters (*Heloderma suspectum*). Ariz. Acad. Sci. 11 (1976 Proc. Suppl.):156.

Sclater, P. L. 1882. [An addition of a Gila monster, *Heloderma suspectum*, to the Society's menagerie.] Proc. Zool. Soc. London:630.

Shannon, F. A. 1953a. Case reports of two Gila monster bites. Herpetologica 9:125-127.

_____. 1953b. Comments on the treatment of reptile poisoning in the Southwest. Southwest. Med. 34:367-373.

_____. 1954. Report on a fatality due to rattlesnake bite. Natural Hist. Misc., Chicago Acad. Sci. 135:1-7.

_____. 1957. Treatment of envenomization by animals of Arizona. Ariz. Med. 14:136-142

_____. 1965. Scorpions, snakes and Gila Monsters. Ariz. Med. 22:968-974

Shaw, C. E. 1948. A note on the food habits of Heloderma suspectum Cope. Herpetologica 4: 145.

_____. 1950. The Gila monster in New Mexico. Herpetologica 6:37-39.

_____. 1964. Beaded lizards -- dreaded but seldom deadly. Zoonooz 37(3):10-15.

_____. 1968. Reproduction of the Gila monster (Heloderma suspectum) at the San Diego Zoo. Zool. Gart. 35:1-6.

Snow, F. H. 1906. Is the Gila monster a poisonous reptile? Trans. Kans. Acad. Sci. 20(2):218-221.

Spring, J. A. 1889. The Gila monster, a personal experience. The Great Divide 1(5):57-58.

Stahnke, H. L. 1950. The food of the Gila monster. Herpetologica 6:103-106.

_____. 1952. A note on the food of the Gila monster, Heloderma suspectum Cope. Herpetologica 8: 64.

_____. 1953. The L-C treatment of venomous bites or stings. Amer. J. Tropical Med. and Hygiene 2:142-143.

_____. 1953. The L-C treatment of venomous bites and stings. Arizona Highways. 29(Feb.):35.

_____. 1974. Cryotherapy: science or witchcraft? Letter to the editor, Arizona Republic, Phoenix. July 24.

Stahnke, H. L., W. A. Heffron and D. L. Lewis. 1970. Bite of the Gila monster. Rocky Mountain Med. J. 67(9):25- 30.

Stephens, F. 1914. Arid California and its animal life. Ann. Report of the Calif. Fish and Game Comm. 23:134.

Stewart, C. 1891. On some points in the anatomy of Heloderma. Proc. Zool. Soc. London:119-121.

Storer, T. I. 1931. Heloderma poisoning in man. Bull. Antivenin Inst. Amer. 5:12-15.

Strong, F. 1915. Lewis Lindsey Dyche. Sci. 41:280-282.

Styblova, Z. and F. Kornalik. 1967. Enzymatic properties of Heloderma suspectum venom. Toxicon 5:139.

Sumichrast, F. 1864. Note on the habits of some Mexican reptiles. Annals and Mag. of Natural History 13 (June):497-500.

Swarth, H. S. 1929. The faunal areas of southern Arizona: a study in animal distribution. Proc. Calif. Acad. Sci. 18(12):267-383.

Taub, A. M. 1963. On the longevity and fecundity of Heloderma horridum horridum. Herpetologica 19:149.

REFERENCES

_____. 1957. I was bitten by a Gila monster. Desert Mag. 20(Sept.):11-12.

Treadwell, G. A. 1888. [Human death alleged from the bite of *Heloderma suspectum*]. Proc. Zool. Soc. London:266.

_____. 1891. The Gila monster. *In* Arizona and some of her friends, the toasts and responses at a complimentary dinner, July 28, 1891, to Hon. John N. Irwin, Governor of Arizona, and H. H. Logan of Phoenix, Arizona. Privately printed.

Tu, A. T., and D. S. Murdock. 1967. Protein nature and some enzymatic properties of the lizard *Heloderma suspectum suspectum* (Gila monster) venom. Comp. Biochem. and Physiol. 22:389-396.

Tyler, A. 1946. On natural auto-antibodies as evidenced by anti-venin in serum and liver extract of the Gila monster. Nat. Acad. Sci. Proc. 32:195-201.

_____. 1954. An auto-antivenin in the Gila monster and its relation to a concept of natural auto-antibodies. Abstracts of Papers: Intern. Conf. Animal Venoms, Amer. Assoc. Advance. Sci. Berkeley, CA:54.

Van Denburgh, J. 1897. Gila monsters venomous. Scientific Amer. 76:373.

_____. 1898. Some experiments with the saliva of the Gila monster. Amer. Phil. Soc. Trans.19:201- 220.

Van Denburgh, J. and J. R. Slevin. 1913. A list of the amphibians and reptiles of Arizona with notes on the species in the collection of the Academy. Proc. Calif. Acad. Sci.(4th series) 3:391-454.

Van Denburgh, J., and O. B. Wight. 1900. On the physiological action of the poisonous secretion of the Gila monster (*Heloderma suspectum*). Amer. J. Physiol. 4:209-238.

Van Duyn, G. 1946. "Gila", a present day monster. Nature Mag. Mar.:147.

Van Pelt, J. 1966. Le monstre Gila. (*Heloderma suspectum* Cope). Zoo 31(4):163-165.

Viaux, F. B. 1939. Monster of the desert. New England Naturalist 4:17-19.

Vick, E. C. 1902. The Gila monster. Country Life in America 1:102.

Vorhies, C. T. 1928. *Heloderma suspectum*, automobile tourists and animal distribution. Sci. 68:182-183.

Vorhies, C. T. 1929. Heloderma suspectum, automobile tourists and animal distribution. Arizona Wild Life 2(Nov.):6.

Wagner, E., R. Smith and F. Slavens. 1976. Breeding the Gila monster (*Heloderma suspectum*) in captivity. Intern. Zoo Yearbook. 16:74-78.

Willey, D. A. 1906. Gila monsters. Scientific Amer. 95:192.

Williamson, M. A. 1973. *Heloderma suspectum*, Pp. 114-117 *In* Symposium on rare and endangered wildlife of the southwestern U. S. (Sept. 22-23, 1972). New Mexico Dept. Game and Fish, Santa Fe.

Woodbury, A. M. 1928. The reptiles of Zion National Park. Copeia 166:14-21.

Woodson, W. D. 1943a. How dangerous is the Gila monster? Desert Mag. 6(Sept.):11-14.

_____. 1943b. Lizards, monsters in minature. Travel Mar. 31: 31.

_____. 1943c. The Gila monster's bite. Frontiers 8(1):19-20.

_____. 1947. Toxicity of *Heloderma* venom. Herpetologica 4:31-33.

_____. 1948. He watches them grow. Pacific Discovery 1(5):15-17.

_____. 1949a. Diseases of *Heloderma*. Herpetologica 5:91.

_____. 1949b. Summary of *Heloderma*'s food habits. Herpetologica 5:91-92.

_____. 1949c. Gila monster in California? Herpetologica 5:151.

_____. 1950. I keep a Gila monster in my home. Desert Mag. 14(Dec).:19-22.

_____. Gila monster. New Mexico Mag. 22(3):19, 33-34.

Yarrow, H. C. 1888. Bite of the Gila monster. Forest and Stream 30 (June):412-423.

Yatkola, D. A. 1976. Fossil *Heloderma* (Reptilia, Helodermatidae). Occas. Papers Mus. Natural Hist. Univ. Kansas 51:1-14.

Zarafonetis, C. J. D., and J. P. Kalas. 1962. Serotonin degradation by homogenates of tissues from *Heloderma horridum*, the Mexican beaded lizard. Nature 195:707.

MASTER'S THESES AND DOCTORAL DISSERTATIONS

Beck, D. D. 1986. The Gila monster in Utah: bioenergetics and natural history considerations. M. S. Thesis, Utah State Univ., Logan. 95p. + tables.

Dengler, A. H. 1967. Some effects of alcoholic beverages on the venoms of *Crotalus atrox* Baird and Girard, *Centruroides sculpturatus* Ewing and *Heloderma suspectum* Cope. M. S. Thesis, Arizona State Univ., Tempe. 49p. + tables.

Farrar, P. W. 1932. The circulatory system of the Gila monster *Heloderma suspectum* Cope. M. S. Thesis, Univ. of Arizona, Tucson. 50p. + tables.

Fawcett, J. R. 1949. Some physiological effects of Gila Monster venom on mammals. M. A. Thesis, Arizona State College, Tempe. 104p. + tables.

Lardner, P. J. 1969. Diurnal and seasonal locomotory activity in the Gila Monster, *Heloderma suspectum* Cope. PhD Diss. Univ. of Arizona, Tucson. 99p. + tables.

Maarsingh, W. E. 1950. The effect of certain environmental stimuli on the coat color of the Gila Monster. M. A. Thesis. Arizona State College, Tempe. 176p + tables.

Porzer-Kepner, L. M. 1981. Movement, behavior, and body temperature of the Gila monster (*Heloderma suspectum*) in Queen Creek, Pinal County, Arizona. M. S. Thesis, Arizona State Univ., Tempe. 100 p. + tables.

GOVERNMENT CONTRACT STUDIES

Beck, D. D. 1982. Preliminary investigation of the banded Gila monster (*Heloderma suspectum cinctum*) in southwestern Utah. Report to the Utah Nongame Division of Wildl. Resour. 11p.

Coombs, E. 1977. Wildlife observations of the hot desert region, Washington County, Utah, with emphasis on reptilian species and their habitat in relation to livestock grazing. Utah Div. Wildl. Res. Rep. contribution to USDI /BLM Utah State Off. Contract No. YA-512-CT 6-102. 204p.

Cross, J. C. 1977. Preliminary herpetological inventory for the Bureau of Land Management, Safford District. Final Report P. O. No. AZ040-PH6-548. 142p.

_____. 1978. Annotated literature review on the ecology of the Gila Monster (*Heloderma suspectum*). Accompaniment to U. S. Bur. Reclam. Contract 8-07-32- V0040. 64p. + addendum.

_____. 1979. Impacts of the Salt-Gila Aqueduct, Central Arizona Project, on the Gila Monster (*Heloderma suspectum*) and suggested mitigation plans. U. S. Bur. of Reclamation Contract No. 8-07-32-V0040. 52p.

Lowe, C. H., Jr. and T. B. Johnson. 1976. A survey of the reptiles and amphibians of the Fort Bowie National Historic Site, Pp. 77-120 *In* Technical Report No. 2, Survey of the vertebrate fauna, Fort Bowie National Historic Site. Coop. Nat. Park Res. Studies Unit, Univ. of Ariz. Contrib. No. CPSU/UA 005/4. (P.O. No. PX8100- 6-0031).

Minckley, W. L. 1972. Herpetefauna of the Orme, Buttes, Charleston, and Hooker Reservoir Sites, Arizona-New Mexico. DI-BR-CAP-CBIO-72-2. 40p.

Ohmart, R. D. 1976. Field studies of the nongame mammals birds, herpetofauna, and vegetation analysis of the proposed Salt-Gila Aqueduct. DI-BR-CAP-CBIO-76-4. 76p.

Ohmart, R. D., L. J. Vitt and R. C. Van Loben Sels. 1975. The herpetefauna of the proposed Orme Dam Site. DI-BR- CAP-CBIO-75-1. 57p.

Vitt, L., J. R. C. Van Loben Sels and R. D. Ohmart. 1976. The herpetofauna of the Buttes Dam Site. DI-BR-CAP- CBIO-76-8. 17p.

ACKNOWLEDGEMENTS

Our discussion of Gila monster biology is based on the knowledge of many people. In this regard we are especially indebted to the comprehensive *The Gila Monster and Its Allies* by Charles M. Bogert and Rafael Martin Del Campo published as a Bulletin of the American Museum of Natural History. While appearing in 1956 and now somewhat dated, this work proved an invaluable aid for its summary of almost everything known or written about Gila monsters at that time. More recent studies of special value are Lauren Porzer-Kepner's Master's Thesis on *Movement, Behavior, and Body Temperature of the Gila Monster* (Heloderma suspectum) *in Queen Creek, Pinal County, Arizona,* and Dan Beck's monograph *Ecology and Behavior of the Gila Monster in Southwestern Utah.* Also of great value was the comprehensive discussion of the Gila monster in the Arizona Game and Fish Department's excellent book, *The Venomous Reptiles of Arizona* by Charles H. Lowe, Cecil Schwalbe and Terry Johnson. We make no claim to being herpetologists or Gila monster experts and are therefore especially grateful to Mr. Howard Lawler, Curator of Herpetology at the Arizona-Sonora Desert Museum, for graciously consenting to be our technical advisor and reviewing the natural history portion of the book. Also assisting with various aspects of the book were Mr. John Annerino; Mr. Randy Babb, Environmental-Education Officer, Arizona Game and Fish Dept.; Mr. John Bidle, Law Enforcement Officer, Arizona Game and Fish Dept.; Dr. Charles M. Bogert; Dr. Tom Boggess III, Kachina Animal Hospital; Ms. Evelyn Boren; Ms. Jenny Cashman, University of Arizona; Ms. Sandy Cates, Adobe Mountain Animal Rehabilitation Center, Arizona Game and Fish Dept.; Dr. Monte Cazier, Arizona State University; Mr. John Conneally, Permit Coordinator, Arizona Game and Fish Dept.; Dr. Jim Dawson; Dr. Bernard L. Fontana, University of Arizona Library; Mr. Tom Gatz, Environmental Division, Bureau of Reclamation; Mr. Bruce Hamana, Executive Director, Gila River Indian Community; Mrs. Rosemary Henderson; Mr. Jim Hills, Arizona Sonora Desert Museum; Dr. John Hubbard, New Mexico Dept. Game and Fish; Mr. John Johnson, Arizona Military Museum; Mr. Terry Johnson, Nongame Branch Supervisor, Arizona Game and Fish Dept.; Mr. K. Bruce Jones, Bureau of Land Management; Mr. William Kepner, U. S. Environmental Protection Agency; Ms. Anne Kessell, Buckhorn Mineral Baths; Mr. Mario Nick Klimiades, Librarian/Archivist, The Heard Museum; Dr. Donald B. Kunkel, Medical Director, Samaritan Regional Poison Center; Ms. Lauren Pozner-Kepner; Mr. John Laird, Curator, Gila Bend Museum;

Dr. Jim MacMahon, Dept. of Biology, Utah State University; Ms. Janet Michaelieu, Librarian, Central Arizona Division of the Arizona Historical Society; Dr. W. L. Minckley, Arizona State University; Mr. Byron D. Nelson, Principal Gila Bend High School; Mr. Larry Nienaber, Custodian, Animal Research Laboratory; Dr. Robert Ohmart, Arizona State University; Mr. Charles Painter, New Mexico Dept. of Game and Fish; Dr. Amadeo Rea; Dr. Mike Robinson; Mr. Rod Roeske; Mr. Budge Ruffner; Dr. Findlay E. Russell, College of Pharmacy, University of Arizona; Mr. M. H. (Dutch) Salmon; Dr. Cecil Schwalbe, University of Arizona; Mr. Harley Shaw; Dr. Wade Sherbrooke, Southwest Research Station, Resident Director American Museum of Natural History; Dr. Norm Smith, University of Arizona; Mr. Barry Spicer, Arizona Game and Fish Dept.; Mr. Don Vance, Law Enforcement Supervisor, Arizona Game and Fish Dept.; Dr. Tom Vandevender, Arizona-Sonora Desert Museum; Dr. Laurie Vitt, Herpetology Dept., University of Oklahoma; Dr. Glenn Walsberg, Arizona State University; Mr. Tom Waddell, Arizona Game and Fish Dept.

Special thanks also to Dr Cecil Schwalbe, University of Arizona herpetologist, for his editorial corrections of some biological information in the first edition.

INSTITUTIONS CONTACTED: Arizona Game and Fish Department, Phoenix; Arizona Historical Foundation, A.S.U., Tempe; Arizona Historical Society, Tucson; Arizona Historical Society, Central Arizona Division, Phoenix; Arizona Military Museum, Phoenix; Arizona Museum, Phoenix; Arizona-Sonora Desert Museum, Tucson; Arizona State Museum and Archives, Capitol Bldg, Phoenix; Arizona State University Library and Archives, Tempe; Gila River Arts and Crafts, Sacaton; Heard Museum, Phoenix; Phoenix Zoo; Pueblo Grande Museum, Phoenix; University of Arizona Library, Tucson; Sharlot Hall Museum, Prescott

INDEX

About the authors: Both writers have been prowling around the Southwest longer than they care to remember. David E. Brown worked as a wildlife biologist for the Arizona Game and Fish Department for 27 years, and Neil Carmony was a chemist with the Water Resources Division of the U.S. Geological Survey for 17 years. Their interest in natural history has resulted in several books on wildlife and outdoor adventure including the following titles which are also available through High-Lonesome Books:

Tales From Tiburon, 1983, Southwest Natural History Association, $10.00.

The Wolf in the Southwest, 1983, University of Arizona Press, $13.00.

The Grizzly in the Southwest, 1985, University of Oklahoma Press, $25.00.

Arizona Game Birds, 1989, University of Arizona Press, $20.00.

Aldo Leopold's Wilderness, 1990, Stackpole Books, $19.00.

Mexican Game Trails, 1991, University of Oklahoma Press, $25.00.

HIGH-LONESOME BOOKS

"Published in the Greatest Country Out-of-Doors"

At HIGH-LONESOME BOOKS we have a great variety of titles for enthusiasts of the Southwest and the great Outdoors - new, used, and rare books of the following:

Southwest History

Wilderness Adventure

Natural History

Hunting

Sporting Dogs

Mountain Men

Fishing

Country Living

Environment

Our brochure/list is FREE for the asking. Write or call.

HIGH-LONESOME BOOKS
P. O. Box 878
Silver City, New Mexico
88062
505-388-3763

Also, come visit our new bookshop in the country at High-Lonesome Road near Silver City